Practical Guide to the Operational Use of the PKM Machine Gun

By Erik Lawrence

Copyright ©2014 Erik Lawrence

Erik Lawrence
www.vig-sec.com   erik@vig-sec.com

Printed and bound in the United States of America

First printing 2006
Second Printing 2014

ISBN-10: 1-941998-02-X
ISBN-13: 978-1-941998-02-1
EBOOK-ISBN 13: 978-1-941998-21-2
LCCN: Not yet assigned

I0170719

ATTENTION US MILITARY UNITS, US GOVERNMENT AGENCIES AND PROFESSIONAL ORGANIZATIONS: Quantity discounts are available on bulk purchases of this book. Special books or book excerpts can also be created to fit specific needs. For information, please contact:

Erik Lawrence
www.vig-sec.com   erik@vig-sec.com

CREDITS:
Wikipedia contributors, "Main Page," Wikipedia, The Free Encyclopedia,
http://en.wikipedia.org/w/index.php?title=Main_Page&oldid=83971314
(accessed October 7, 2006).

Firearms are potentially dangerous and must be handled responsibly by individuals. The technical information presented in this manual on the use of the PK and PKM Machine Gun reflects the author's research, beliefs, and experiences. The information in this book is presented for academic study only. Neither the author nor the publisher assumes any responsibility for the use or misuse of information contained in this book.

SAFETY NOTICE
Before starting an inspection, ensure the weapon is cleared. Do not manipulate the trigger until the weapon has been cleared of all ammunition. Inspect the chamber to ensure that it is empty and no ammunition is present. Keep the weapon oriented in a safe direction when loading and handling.

AMMUNITION NOTICE- these weapons fires the 7.62 x 54 R (Rimmed/Russian) not the 7.62 x 51 NATO (.308 Winchester). Firing the incorrect ammunition will damage the weapon and possibly injure the operator/assistant operator.

Training should be received from knowledgeable and experienced operators on this particular weapons system. Vigilant Security Services, LLC provides this training and continually perfects its instruction with up-to-date information from actual use.

www.vig-sec.com

PREFACE

This manual is intended to be a reference for those involved in the use, maintenance and instruction of the featured firearm. My aim in writing these manuals is to set the record straight and dispel many of the false assumptions related to the different firearms. The early sections of the manual contain background material on the featured firearm which allows the user to gain the basic building blocks for further education. The firearms featured in these manuals have been used for decades by our allies and enemies, and will be for the foreseeable future, so why are we not experts with them? If I am fighting with the firearm or providing instruction on a firearm, I want to use and know their system better than they do.

The rationale for writing these manuals comes from the fact that there are not libraries of easily accessible references to use in developing your own training system for these firearms. Many of the old military field manuals are decades old and were incorrectly translated by someone who had no idea what the firearm could do, let alone basic firearm knowledge. We started from the ground up and developed the manuals to provide instruction in progressive steps that could be easily grasped and continually referred back to. A good grounding in the basics of firearms, safety, and instruction allows the user to use these manuals to their maximum value. A competent user will find little difficulty in interpreting and applying the information in the manual to their own training program.

The guide goes through the most fundamental parts of the firearm in detail and more advanced techniques are not covered as extensively. With this in mind the user can use these principles and adapt it as needed to their required level of instruction. The emphasis of this guide is in acquiring familiarity with the fundamentals of all firearms and learned competence rather than becoming a firearms guru.

Many of the points in these guides were developed from scratch in theatres of conflict and are continually improved and updated for each edition. I have continually used vetted points from users and professionals in the guides to continually update them to the best known practices for each particular firearm. If it is valid and relevant we will include it in the next edition.

Please note that this guide assumes some familiarity with the basic concepts in firearm safety, gun handling skills, common sense and an ability to process new information. Readers should have knowledge of the difference in calibers, countries of origin, and the knowledge of the priority of the skills needed for development.

I hope you find this work useful and remember that a manual does not replace proper training and hands on experience. Please email comments to erik@vig-sec.com, particularly if you find any errors or glaring omissions.

Erik Lawrence

Table of Contents

PKM
general purpose
MACHINE GUN

Section 1

PK/PKM Operator Manual Introduction

The objective of this manual is to allow the reader to be able to use the PK/PKM and tripod mount system competently. The manual will give the reader background/specifications of the weapon, instruct on its operation, disassembly and assembly, demonstrate correct usage of tripod; detail proper firing procedure; and identify malfunction/misfire procedures. Operator-level maintenance will also be detailed to allow the reader to understand fully and become competent in the use and maintenance of the PKM general-purpose machine gun.

Description

Weapon Specifications
- Mode: Full-automatic only
- Operation: Gas
- Cartridge: 7.62 x 54 mm
- Weight (without tripod or ammunition): 8.4 kg/18.5 lbs.
- Overall length: 119 cm/47 inches
- Cyclic rate of fire: 690-720 rpm
- Sustained rate of fire: 250 rpm
- Combat effective range: 1000m
- Sighting range: 1500 m

Feed
- Ammunition capacity: 50-round soft nylon box, 100- or 200-round metal box
- Non-disintegrating metal belt link (25-round connectable sections)
- Direction: Right to left

Barrel
- Length: 60.3 cm/23.75 inches
- Quick changeable type mechanism
- Muzzle velocity: 825 m/s/2700 fps

Rates of Fire with the PKM

Sustained rate of fire is 100 rounds per minute in bursts of 6 to 9 rounds in 4 to 5 second intervals. It is recommended to change the barrel if firing the sustained rate every 10 minutes.

Rapid rate of fire is 200 rounds per minute in bursts of 6 to 9 rounds in 2 to 3 second intervals. It is recommended to change the barrel if firing the rapid rate every two minutes.

Cyclic rate of fire is the maximum amount of ammunition which can be expended in one minute. It is recommended to change the barrel if firing the cyclic rate every one minute.

Sights
- Front - protected cylindrical post
- Rear - rectangular notch, tangent ramp
- Rear sight graduation - 100-1500 meters in 100-meter increments and battle setting is approximately 330 meters
- Adjustment - front sight for zero only and rear sight for elevation and windage

Action
- Locking feature is a rotary bolt.
- Full automatic from the open bolt
- The trigger type is a spur.
- Safety type is a rotary selector with safe and fire settings.
- Safety location is on the left side above the trigger guard.

PK/PKM Background

Figure 1-1 PKM Machine Gun

The PK family of machine guns are gas-operated, rotating-bolt, open-bolt firing, and fully automatic, belt-fed machine guns.

The original **PK** (*ПУЛЕМЕТ КАЛАШНИКОВА, "Machine gun Kalashnikov"* was a fully automatic machine gun development of the Kalashnikov automatic rifle design. Currently available as the **PKM** (*ПУЛЕМЕТ КАЛАШНИКОВА МОДЕРНИЗИРОВАННЫЙ, Machine gun Kalashnikov Modernized*), the machine gun fires 7.62 x 54R mm standard ammunition. It is equipped with a simple bipod and is designed as a squad-level support weapon also suitable for installation and vehicle mounting. The PKM is generally utilized as an infantry support weapon. Used in this classic role, it provides long-range area fire, supports final protective fires lanes, and can provide anti-aircraft (AA) fire. The PK can also be used in the front firing ports of the BMP. It has an adjustable cyclic rate and an effective range of 1000 meters. Effective range of the gun in the AA role is 600 meters against slow-moving aircraft. Its ammunition is not common to the AK-47 and other Russian weapons carried by infantry units currently. For heavier employment, the **PKMS** model *(ПКМ СТЕПАНОВА, PKM Stepanova,* for the name of the tripod) features a more stable tripod mounting.

The **PKM** and variants are in production in Russia and other former Eastern Bloc countries and currently are exported to many nations. The **PK** and its descendants will continue to see service throughout the world for some time.

There are several variants, and the PK has become a true general-purpose machine gun (GPMG). The following is a list of the variants:

Figure 1-2 PK Machine Gun

- **PK**: *ПУЛЕМЕТ КАЛАШНИКОВА (ПК), Pulemyot Kalashnikova,* Machine gun Kalashnikov. Introduced in 1961, it is the basic gun with a heavy fluted barrel, feed cover constructed from both machined and stamped components, and a plain butt plate. The PK weighs 9 kg/19.8 lbs.

Figure 1-3 PKS Machine Gun

- **PKS:** *Pulemyot Kalashnikova Stankoviy*, the basic gun mounted on a Samozhenkov designed tripod.

Figure 1-4 PKT Machine Gun

- **PKT:** *ПУЛЕМЕТ КАЛАШНИКОВА ТАНКОВЫЙ, Pulemyot Kalashnikova Tankoviy, PK Tank* the tank-mounted version of the PK. Introduced in 1962 for late-model Soviet tanks, turreted armored personnel carriers (APC) and Infantry combat vehicles (ICV). Amphibious scout cars mount it as a coaxial machine gun. The PKT was developed from the PK machine gun; it has a longer and heavier barrel than the PK. However, given the specifics of the PK combat use, Kalashnikov incorporated a number of changes: the barrel weight was increased by 1.2 kg/2.6 lbs. to ensure more intensive fire, the spring of the guiding piston rod was incorporated to reduce the rocking of the barrel and receiver, the gas regulator was manufactured on the principle of a changing gas section to reduce an excessive accumulation of discharged powder gases in combat compartment, the sighting device was replaced by an optical sight, and an electric trigger was incorporated to ensure remotely controlled fire that was attached to the receiver's end plate instead of a buttstock, although it also has an emergency manual trigger. Weight of the weapon with mount without ammunition is 10.5 kg/23.1lb.

Figure 1-5 PKB Machine Gun

- **PKB:** *Pulemyot Kalashnikova na Bronetransportere, Machine gun Kalashnikov* for transporter. Introduced in 1969, the PKB is a general-purpose machine gun mounted on armored personnel carriers. The machine gun is placed on a special mount that connects it to an armored personnel carrier bracket. The PKB mount is metallic. It is outfitted with a swivel to ensure machine gun traverse and sector for its elevation, bracket for cartridge box, frame to connect machine gun with mount, and a bag to collect fired cartridge cases. Weight with mount without ammo is 18.5 kgs/40.7 lbs.

Figure 1-6 PKM Machine Gun

- **PKM:** *ПУЛЕМЕТ КАЛАШНИКОВА МОДЕРНИЗИРОВАННЫЙ, Pulemyot Kalashnikova Modernizrovee,* Machine gun Kalashnikov Modernized. Introduced in 1969, a lightened and improved PK. It utilizes a lighter un-fluted barrel, and excess metal has been machined away to lower the weight to 8.4 kg/18.5lb.

NOTE: the PKM barrel has no grooves like the PK barrel, and the feed-tray cover is a single piece of stamped material.

Figure 1-7 PKMS Machine Gun

- **PKMS:** *ПУЛЕМЕТ КАЛАШНИКОВА МОДЕРНИЗИРОВАННЫЙ Степанова*, Machine gun Kalashnikov Modernized, Stepanova. PKM mounted on a Stepanova-designed lighter design tripod mount. Weight of the tripod is 4.5 kg/10 lbs. The lightweight tripod provides a stable platform for very accurate ground fire and provides the ability to fire as an anti-aircraft gun out to 600 meters.

Figure 1-8 PKMT Machine Gun

- **PKMT:** *ПУЛЕМЕТ КАЛАШНИКОВА МОДЕРНИЗИРОВАННЫЙ ТАНКОВЫЙ, Pulemyot Kalashnikova Modernizrovee Tankoviy.* Introduced in 1969, PK Modernized Tank, the coaxial variant of the standard PKM. The sights, stock, tripod, and trigger mechanism have been removed for use in the tank mode. A heavier barrel is affixed, and it is equipped with a solenoid for firing. The PKMT is slightly heavier than the PKT.

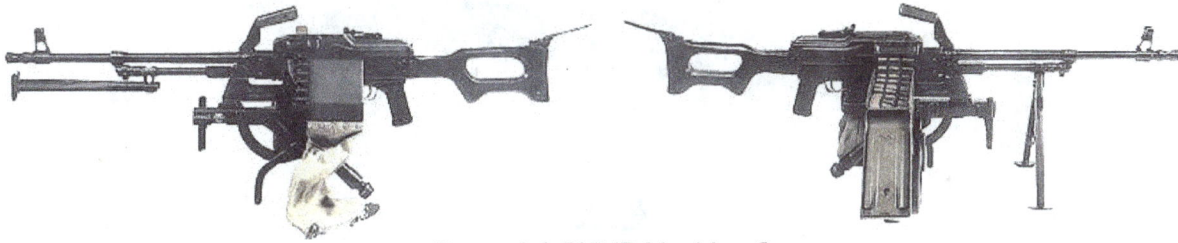

Figure 1-9 PKMB Machine Gun

- **PKMB:** Pulemyot Kalashnikova na Bronetransportere, Machine gun Kalashnikov Modernized for Transporter. PKM specialized mount for use from armored personnel carriers. After upgrading the PK machine gun, it was designated the PKM, and the armored personnel carrier machine gun version was designated the PKMB. The PKB differs from the PKMB in weight. Weight of the weapon with mount without ammo is 17.5 kg/38.5 lbs.

Figure 1-10 PKMSN2 Machine Gun

- **PKMSN2:** Model fits modern **NSPU** night sights for low-visibility operations. Weight of the weapon with mount and NSPU is 13.8 kg/30.4 lbs.

Figure 1-11 PKP (Pecheneg) Machine Gun

- **PKP**: *ПУЛЕМЕТ КАЛАШНИКОВА Печенег, Pulemyot Kalashnikova Pecheneg.* It was named *Pecheneg* for an ancient aggressive tribe who lived in what later became Russia/Ukraine. Introduced in 2003, PKP, the modernized PK machine gun with a heavier, non-removable forced air cooling barrel with radial cooling fins and a handle which eliminates the mirage effect from hot gases and keeps the barrel cooler. The caliber is 7.62x54R, weight is 19 lbs/8.7kg without the tripod, weight with the tripod is 28 lbs/12.7kg, overall length is 45"/1155mm, the barrel length is 26"/658mm and the rate of fire is 650 rpm. The military designation of the PKP is 6P41/6P41N (N with a night vision sight). The PKP is currently in use by Russian Spetsnaz and other troops in small numbers. The PKP is capable of mounting a telescopic sight with the standard Russian reticle which increases accuracy and versatility. All previous PK/PKM accessories will work with the PKP.

Figure 1-12 PKP Barrel

Barrel- Its key difference from the original PK design is the barrel, which is not intended to be replaced in the field but can be removed for inspection and maintenance. The barrel is heavier than that of the standard PKM, and has radial cooling fins. The barrel is enclosed in a steel jacket, which runs up to the muzzle to provide forced air cooling like a Lewis machine gun of WWI. Cooling air enters the jacket through oval windows at the rear of the jacket and exits at the muzzle. Early versions of the PKP had the standard PKM-type flash hider, which resulted in a significant muzzle blast once the gun is warmed up but current production PKPs have a special flash hider which eliminates this problem. At the rear of the jacket there is a carrying handle permanently attached to it. This handle has a characteristic elongated profile, as it is also intended to protect the line of sight from mirages generated by the hot barrel.

Figure 1-13 PKP Bipod

Bipod- The PKP's bipod is changed from the standard PK design as the location of the integral, non-removable folding bipod is placed near the muzzle. This feature supposedly improves stability and long-range accuracy when firing from the bipod but it also limits the arc of fire without moving the position of bipod or shooter. Another consequence of such placement is that the PKP is more difficult if you had to fire from the shoulder or the hip, as it does not have a handguard (folded back bipod on PKMs) as it is located too far forward to be used to hold the gun.

POLAND

UKM-2000 P Machine Gun - <mark>7.62x51mm NATO</mark>

- The UKM-2000 P chambers the 7.62×51mm NATO round not the standard PK caliber of 7.62x54R. This modernized version of the UKM-2000 D was developed when Poland joined NATO and needed a GPMG which fires NATO standard ammunition. It is a gas-operated, air-cooled, belt-fed, fully automatic machine gun. It weighs 18.4 lbs/8.4kg, overall length is 47"/1203mm and the barrel length is 21"/540mm.

Figure 1-14 UKM-2000 P

UKM-2000 D Machine Gun - <mark>7.62x51mm NATO</mark>

- The UKM-2000 D chambers the 7.62×51mm NATO round not the standard PK caliber of 7.62x54R. This weapon was developed when Poland joined NATO and needed a GPMG which fires NATO standard ammunition. It is a gas-operated, air-cooled, belt-fed, fully automatic machine gun. It weighs 19.6 lbs/8.9kg, overall length is 47"/1203mm and the barrel length is 21"/540mm.

Figure 1-15 UKM-2000 D

UKM-2000 C (Tank) Machine Gun - <mark>7.62x51mm NATO</mark>

- The UKM-2000 C chambers the 7.62×51mm NATO round not the standard PK caliber of 7.62x54R. This weapon was developed when Poland joined NATO and needed a GPMG which fires NATO standard ammunition. It is a gas-operated, air-cooled, belt-fed, fully automatic machine gun designed for mounting on tanks and other armored vehicles. It weighs 23 lbs/10.5kg, overall length is 43"/1100mm and the barrel length is 25"/635mm and fires remotely.

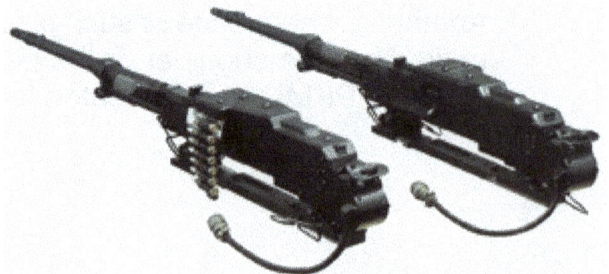
Figure 1-16 UKM-2000 C

Figure 1-17 M84 GP Machine Gun

- **M84**: The **Zastava (Yugoslavian manufacturer) M84** is a general purpose machine gun developed in Yugoslavia during the 1980s. The M84 is based on the Russian PK machine gun. The M84 chambers the 7.62×54mmR round. It is a gas-operated, air-cooled, belt-fed, fully automatic machine gun. It weighs 24 lbs/11kg, overall length is 46'/1175mm and the barrel length is 26"/658mm. It differs from the PK-series in that it has a solid wooden stock and an unfluted barrel. It is also configured for tripod mounting (PKS) and comes with a scope mount (PKMSN). PKM accessories and links are used with this weapon system.

Figure 1-18 M86 Coaxial Machine Gun

The **M86** variant is based on the PKT, and is designed to mount as a coaxial weapon on tanks and other combat vehicles. The stock, bipod, and iron sights are omitted from this version, and it includes a heavier barrel with an electric trigger.

General Characteristics

PK/PKM Construction

Like all other true machine guns, the PK/PKM fires from an open bolt. Despite that feature, the basic operating principle follows the familiar Kalashnikov pattern. The PK has a rotating bolt with two locking lugs, similar to the AK bolt. The PK's bolt is larger and more robust; it has a larger bolt face to accept a 7.62 mm rimmed round and a single claw extractor similar to the AK assault rifles.

Because the PK fires from an open bolt, the firing pin is temporarily fixed on the bolt carrier. The firing pin can be moved with the bolt, but while the bolt is rotating along its carrier guideway, the firing pin stays locked on the bolt carrier. It will project and strike a primer while the bolt rotates to engage on the locking lugs. The PK's bolt carrier is somewhat similar to the AK slide, except it is turned upside down, it is bigger and heavier, and has a less complex shape. The PK is gas operating with a long stroke piston, i.e., the gas piston is permanently mounted on the bolt carrier and moves with it. The gas piston and its rod are chrome-plated for better corrosion resistance and pivoted on the bolt carrier. The hinge allows for slight bending of the carrier/gas piston while it is removed/installed. Not all PK series machine guns have a slide buffer, but Hungarian and Yugoslavian made ones do. If you have examined buffers in other machine guns, the buffer may be a fancy name for 1/4 inch thick plate of fiber-reinforced reddish plastic placed at the rear end of the recoil spring guide. The purpose is to reduce bolt carrier recoil by preventing a straight contact between the bolt carrier and the receiver, and it also helps with removing and installing the recoil spring guide. The PK family has the gas piston and tube mounted beneath the barrel. The gas tube is fixed on the receiver by a spring steel latch, and it can be separated for cleaning.

The gas block is mounted permanently on the barrel and connected to the gas tube via the gas regulator. The infantry versions have an exhaust type, three-position regulator. Position "1" is a basic setting, which is used with a clean gun, and the next positions "2" and "3" are used when the action gets dirtier. The gas regulator can be adjusted by using a cartridge or empty case as a tool. Theoretical cyclic rate is 650 rpm, according Russian literature. Because the PK action has no proper buffering device, which is required for higher cyclic rates, increasing the cyclic rate with regulator settings is not recommended because it increases the wear of the receiver and operating parts and will reduce the service life of the gun. The PKT- and PKB-type machine guns have a different "Venturi" type gas regulator, which doesn't exhaust fumes to the vehicle's interior.

The receiver is a U-section stamped from 1.5 mm sheet steel and assembled by riveting and spot welding. The receiver has double walls made from two 1.5 mm plates welded one upon another. The receiver top's cover is stamped from sheet steel and hinged at the front to the receiver and locked at the back with a spring-loaded latch. The ejector is similar to the AK's and riveted inside the receiver. The PK/PKM ejects empty cases through the ejection port located on the left side of the receiver. The ejection port has a spring-loaded dust cover. With the proper gas-selector setting, the ejection cycle is not as violent as the AK cycle, and the PK won't damage ejected cases. The PK expels empty cases straight to the left at a distance of about 1 meter.

The barrel extension is riveted on the front of the receiver in the AKM manner. The barrel extension mounts the gas-piston tube and includes the quick-change barrel-locking mechanism borrowed from the SG43/SGM machine gun. The barrel extension has a straight boring to accept a cylindrical-mounting piece of barrel and two indexing studs to keep the barrel in the right position. A horizontally sliding locking latch fixes the barrel to the receiver.

The barrel is the easiest way to distinguish the PK and its modernized variation, the PKM. The PK has a heavier, fluted barrel, while the PKM barrel is lighter (it weighs 2.35 kg / 5.1 lbs. and has no longitudinal grooves). The armored vehicle variations PKT/PKTM and PKB/PKBM have even heavier barrels, better suited to the sustained fire role. Like most other small arms of Soviet origin, the PK/PKM family barrels have chrome-plated bores and chambers. They are chromed due to the practice of using corrosive primers, and chroming greatly assist in the cleaning of the bore. The PKM bore has four grooves with a right-hand twist of one turn in 225mm/10 inches. The barrel length is 602mm/23.7 inches, which doesn't include the flash hider or any other muzzle device. The muzzle has left-hand metric M18 x 1.5 threads to mount a flash hider or a blank firing adapter. An AK-type spring-loaded plunger holds the muzzle device in the correct position. There exists at least two different PK-series flash hiders. The most common type is similar to the M14 flash hider with five longitudinal slots. The more recent model is shorter and conical, also having five slots. The barrel has a pivoting handle, which can be used as a lever to assist the barrel out from its housing and carrying a hot weapon.

The trigger housing is mounted permanently underneath the receiver, and it includes the trigger guard. The trigger mechanism, very similar to the RPD, squad automatic weapon, is simple and also very similar to many submachine guns firing from an open bolt. The rotating safety catch located on the left side of trigger housing has two settings: safe and full-auto. No provision for semi-automatic fire, generally considered unneeded in general purpose machine guns.

The PK/PKM machine guns will usually appear with a skeletonized buttstock made from laminated wood. However, there is no rule without a few exceptions. Some examples of Bulgarian-made PK machine guns have appeared with plastic buttstocks, the Chinese Type 80 has a skeletonized buttstock, made from solid wood, and the Yugo M84 also has a solid wood buttstock. Refer to Appendix A for factory marks of various countries. The PK and PKM have steel butt plates with a trapdoor compartment for cleaning gear. The PKM has a steel shoulder strap. An integral oiler is located on the top of the buttstock. Pistol grip and barrel handle grip plates are usually made from reddish bakelite-type plastic material.

Like most other small arms of Soviet and Warsaw Pact origin, the PK/PKM series machine guns will usually feature a black baked-enamel finish. Some other examples have a blued or manganese phosphate (parkerized) finish.

PK/PKM Feeding Mechanism

A belt-fed machine gun firing rimmed ammunition has a more complicated feeding mechanism than its counterpart chambered for a rimless cartridge. Russians/Soviet have used rimmed 7.62 x 54mm R cartridges for more than 100 years, so they have a lot of experience in designing belt-fed mechanisms for rimmed cartridges. Russian-designed belt-fed ground machine guns, chambered for the 7.62mm rimmed round, include the Degtyarev-designed DS-39, RP-46 based on a magazine-feed DPM light machine gun, Goryunov-designed SG-43, and SGM, to name only those entered in service. There was also a series of fast-firing, belt-fed ShKAS (Shpitalniy-Komaritsky) aircraft machine guns with an 1800 rpm rate of fire.

The PK series belt-fed mechanism, which is located over the breech block, includes some similarities to the RP-46 and Goryunov designs. The double-hooked cartridge gripper is similar to one used in SG 43 and SGM machine guns. Also, the double receiver covers, the feed cover which includes the feed tray and the top cover, are similar to the Goryunov's. The spring-loaded depressing arm is a take-off from the RP-46.

The PK family utilizes non-disintegrating, closed-pocket metallic belts. It is the same as used with the Soviet Maxims, the RP-46, and SG43/SGM machine guns. The PK belts will usually appear in four lengths; 25, 100, 200 and 250 rounds. The 100-round belts are used with a small belt box that can be snapped beneath the receiver. In light machine gun configuration, the 100-round belt with that assault box is usually employed. The 200-round and 250-round belts will fit in a bigger belt box, which is the same as is used with the Goryunovs. The 250-round belt box is a logical choice if fired from the tripod, and it can be readily mounted on the tripod. Both Russian/Soviet belt boxes are stamped from sheet aluminum. The 250-round type is all aluminum, while the 100-round box has an aluminum frame with a steel cover. Both types have canvas carry handles.

The "pull-off" type belts are usually used with machine guns chambered for rimmed rounds typically. The PK series belt-fed mechanism works as follows: The belt comes to the feed tray from the right side of the PK. The feed tray is located over the chamber, and cartridges are pulled out from the belt rearwards. While the bolt carrier starts its withdraw after a shot is fired, the cartridge gripper pulls the next cartridge from the belt, and the bolt carrier movement activates the feed pawl to move leftwards to pull the belt inwards. After traveling about 9cm backwards, the cartridge stops at the feed cam mounted on the top cover and is dropped over the feed lips of the feed tray by a spring-loaded depressing arm. Just before that action the ejector expels an empty case through a spring-loaded ejection port on left side of receiver. The bolt carrier continues its withdraw for about 4cm. When the forward motion begins, the bolt pushes the fresh round towards the chamber, and the bolt carrier movement forces the feed pawl to move back to the right. A holding pawl located on the top cover retains the belt.

PK/PKM Ammunition

The 7.62 x 54mm Russian/Rimmed ammunition used by the PK/PKM is produced by Russia, former Soviet republics, China, and many different European countries. The 7.62 x 54mm R cartridges will be encountered in both brass and steel cases; however, steel cases are more prolific. The <u>7.62mm</u> is the diameter of the bullet, <u>54mm</u> is the length of the case, and <u>R</u> represents Russian or Rimmed.

The following is a brief list of the different types of ammunition and their uses:

- Steel core ball - for use against light material targets, personnel, or training. The steel core ball weighs 148 grains and has a muzzle velocity of 825 m/s (2700 fps). No tip markings, or some are yellow tipped.

Figure 1-19 Steel core ammunition

- Steel core ball - for use against light material targets, personnel, or training. The steel core ball weighs 182 grains and has a muzzle velocity of 825 m/s (2700 fps). Tip markings on the bullet are yellow tipped.

- Tracer - for observation of fire, incendiary effects, signaling, and use during training. Green-tipped marking denotes the green trace when fired.

Figure 1-20 Tracer ammunition

- Armor piercing - for use against lightly armored targets where armor-piercing effects are desired. Black tipped marking.

Figure 1-21 Armor-piercing ammunition

- Armor piercing-incendiary - for desired armor-piercing effects combined with fire producing/incendiary effects. Tip markings are Black and Red or Purple.

- Blank - for use during training when simulating live fire. If blanks are to be fired from the PKM machine gun, a blank adapter must first be fitted to the muzzle. Without the blank adapter, insufficient gas pressure is generated to cycle the weapon properly. Crimped purple nose.

Figure 1-22 Blank ammunition

Ammunition Identification

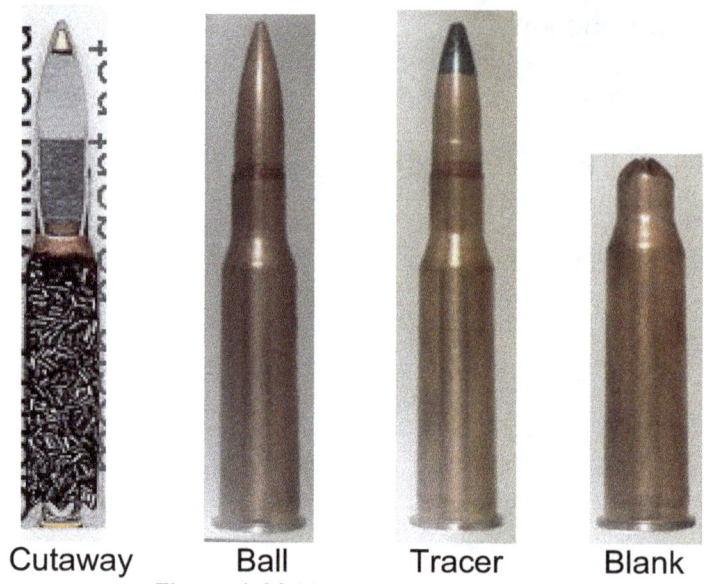

| Cutaway | Ball | Tracer | Blank |

Figure 1-23 Various ammunition examples

Caliber, mm	Case	Bullet type	Bullet, wt. Gram/grain	Primer Type	Description
7.62 x 54R	Bimetal	Bimetal	9.6/148	Berdan	Steel Core
7.62 x 54R	Bimetal	Tracer T-46	9.65/149	Berdan	Tracer Bullet
7.62 x 54R	Bimetal	None	None	Berdan	Blank

7.62 x 54 R Ballistic Chart

7.62 x 54 R 148 grain ball ammunition

BC: 0.398   CALIBER: 0.308 inch/7.62mm   WEIGHT: 148 grain/9.6 grams

Muzzle Velocity: 2700 ft/s

WS: 10 mph

Temperature: 59 °F   Barometric Pressure: 29.92 in Hg

Range	Bullet Drop		Wind		Lead	
(meters)	(inches)	(moa)	(inches)	(moa)	(inches)	(moa)
100	6.4	5.6	1.0	0.9	22.4	19.5
200	7.4	3.2	4.4	1.9	47.0	20.5
300	-0.0	-0.0	10.4	3.0	74.4	21.6
400	-17.8	-3.9	19.5	4.2	104.8	22.9
500	-48.5	-8.5	32.1	5.6	138.7	24.2
600	-95.3	-13.9	48.8	7.1	176.8	25.7
700	-162.5	-20.3	70.1	8.7	219.4	27.4
800	-254.8	-27.8	96.1	10.5	266.7	29.1
900	-377.9	-36.7	126.6	12.3	318.5	30.9
1000	-537.2	-46.9	161.1	14.1	374.3	32.7
1100	-737.7	-58.6	198.9	15.8	433.5	34.4
1200	-984.2	-71.6	239.8	17.5	495.7	36.1
1300	-1281.4	-86.1	283.7	19.1	560.9	37.7
1400	-1633.7	-101.9	330.3	20.6	628.8	39.2
1500	-2046.0	-119.1	379.7	22.1	699.6	40.7

7.62 x 54 R Ballistic chart

NOTE: Minute of Angle (MOA): The term Minute of Angle, referred to as MOA, is actually a unit of measure dealing with circles found in surveying, navigation and mathematics. One Minute of Angle is 1/60th of one degree of a circle. A circle has 360 degrees, and 21,600 Minutes of Angle are in a circle.

If you were to look at a circle which has a radius of 100 yards and project lines out from the center in Minute of Angle increments, you would find that at 100 yards away from the center of the circle, the distance between the Minute of Angle lines would be 1.0472 inches.

Over time, one Minute of Angle at 100 yards has been rounded off to one inch and has become a standard unit of measurement for bullet trajectory calculations, comparisons, accuracy levels, and the sighting-in of firearms.

The chart below illustrates the Minute of Angle concept and plots what one, two, and three Minutes of Angle would be at various distances.

One, Two and Three Minute of Angle (MOA) Chart

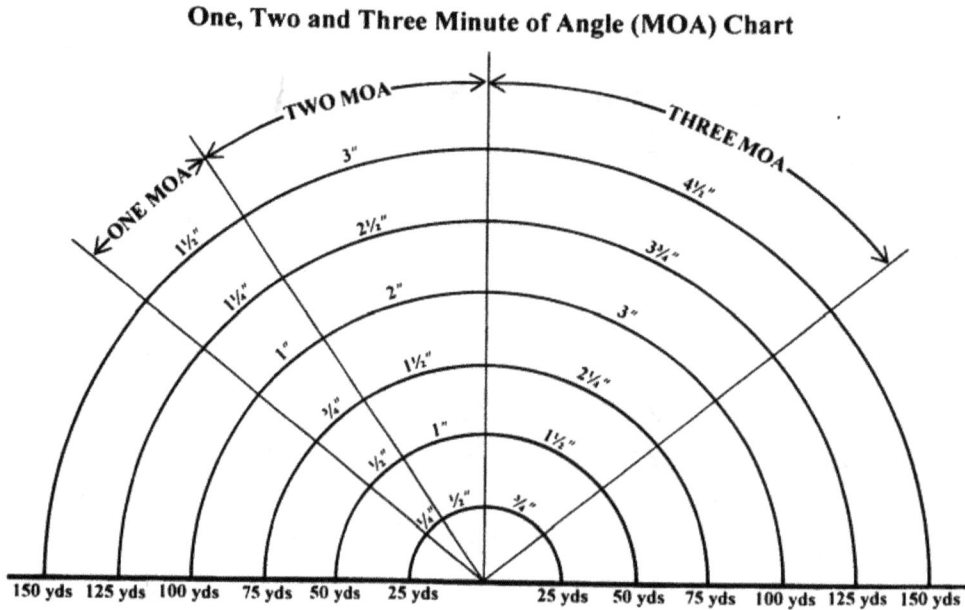

150 yds 125 yds 100 yds 75 yds 50 yds 25 yds   25 yds 50 yds 75 yds 100 yds 125 yds 150 yds

The chart below shows another viewpoint of how Minute of Angle measurements apply to firearms and accuracy. Frequently, a weapon's accuracy is described as being able to fire groups that are less than one Minute of Angle at 100 yards. This would mean that if the shooter fired five rounds at a target 100 yards away and used correct sight alignment, the group would measure less than one inch.

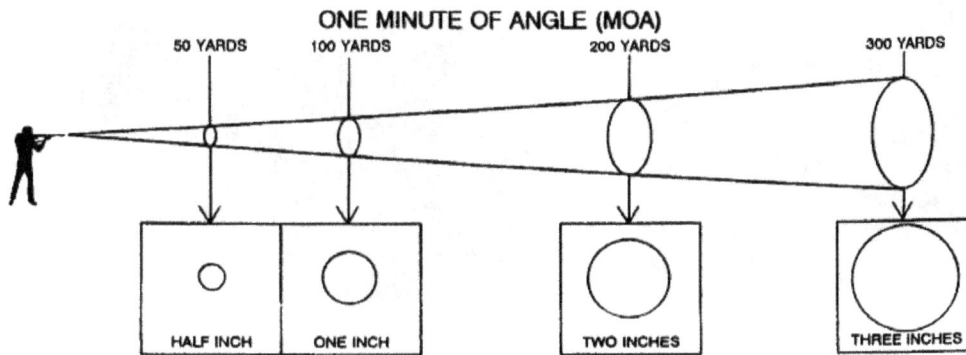

ONE MINUTE OF ANGLE (MOA)

| 50 YARDS | 100 YARDS | | 200 YARDS | 300 YARDS |

| HALF INCH | ONE INCH | TWO INCHES | THREE INCHES |

PK/PKM Ammunition Containers and Links

The weapon is fed by non-disintegrating metal link belts. Current belts are joined 25-round sections. Link containers to hold the ammunition belts securely to the bottom of the weapon or onto the tripod include:

Figure 1-24a VSS designed and constructed 50-round soft ammo carriers

- 50-round soft nylon, zippered bottom to load as the M249 SAW 100-round soft pouch.

Figure 1-24b VSS designed and constructed 100-round soft ammo carriers

- 100-round soft nylon, zippered side to load.

Figure 1-25 100-round standard metal ammo carriers

- 100-round metal box, measures 3.5" width x 5.5" depth x 9.5" length (90mm W x 140mm D x 240mm L), and weighs 3.5 kg/7.8 lbs fully loaded.

Figure 1-26 250-round standard metal ammo carrier

- 250-round metal boxes, measures 3.5" width x 10.5" depth x 10.5" length (90mm W x 270mm D x 270mm L), and weighs 8.75 kg/19 lbs. fully loaded.

| Hungarian packaging | Polish packaging | Czech packaging |

Figure 1-27 Various ammunition packaging

Typical packaging in two 440-round metal cans in a wooden case for a total of 880 rounds. The individual rounds will be packaged in paper in quantities of 20 rounds.

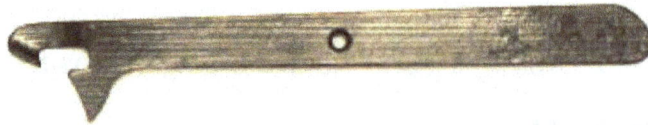

Figure 1-28 Ammunition can opener

Metal can opener used to open the sardine style metal cans. One opener will be in each wooden crate that contains the two metal ammo cans. Without it, opening the cans is quite an adventure; we have used Leatherman, chisels, and bayonets. If using a bayonet or other non designed can opener, be careful not to beat a bayonet tip into one of the primers.

Blank Firing Adapter

The Blank Firing Adapter (BFA) replaces the flash suppressor to allow for the firing of blanks in training exercises.

Figure 1-29 Blank fire accessories
Left - blank firing adapter, Right - live round restrictor

Installing the blank firing adapter-

1. To install the blank firing adapter ensure the weapon has been properly cleared.

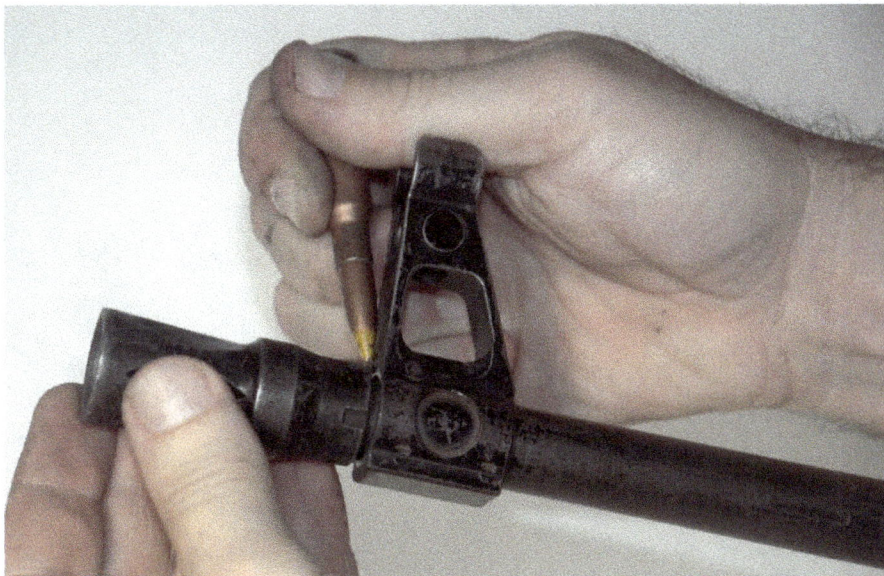

Figure 1-30 Flash suppressor removal

2. Depress the spring-loaded detent and unscrew (reverse threaded-right direction) the birdcage muzzle break. Figure 1-30.

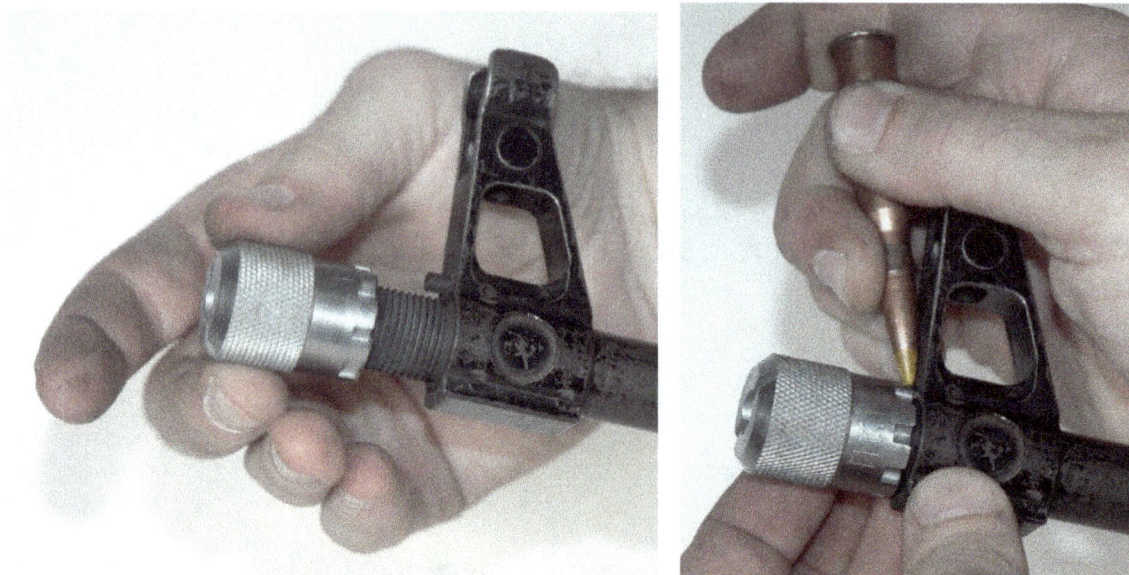

Figure 1-31 Blank firing adapter installation

3. Then screw (reverse threaded-left turn direction) the adapter on and depress the spring-loaded detent until tight and release the detent to fit one of the cutouts on the adapter. Figure 1-31.

Installing the live-round restrictor for using the PKM for blank firing-

1. To install the live round restrictor, ensure the weapon has been properly cleared.

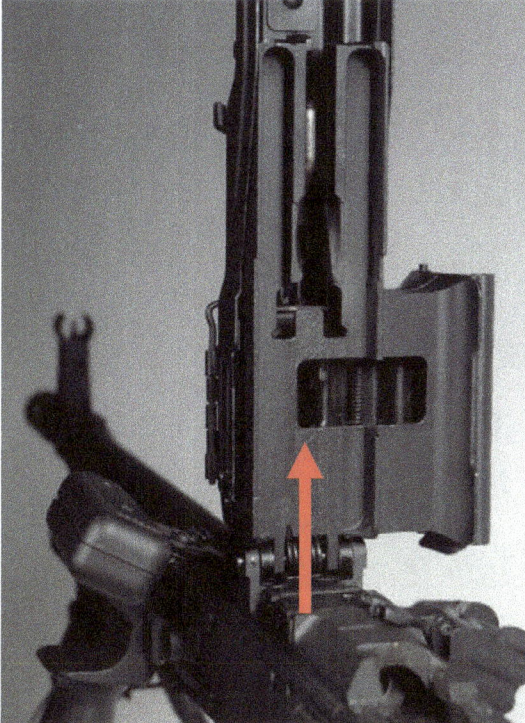

Figure 1-32a

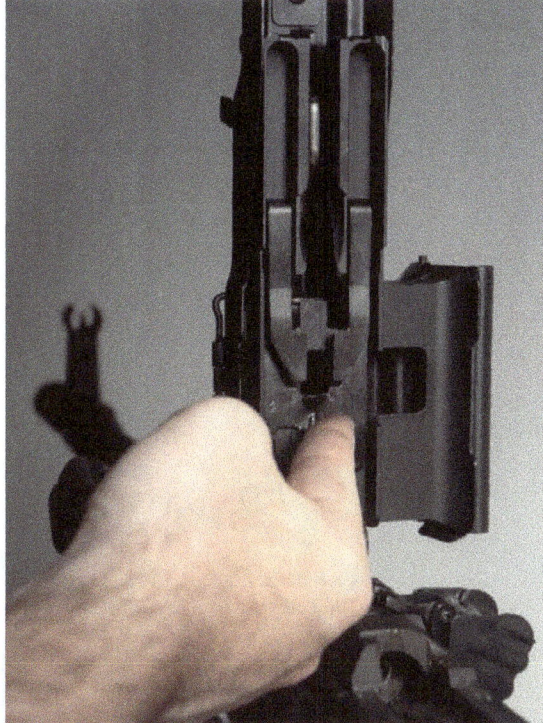

Figure 1-32b

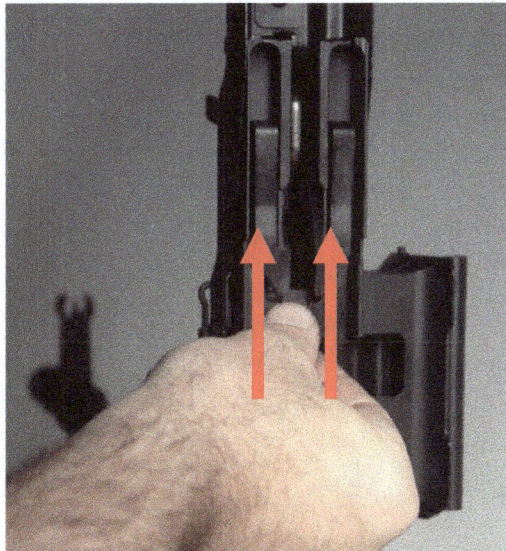

Figure 1-32c Live round restrictor installation

2. Fully open the feed-tray cover and feed tray to expose the bottom of the feed tray. Note the orientation of the restrictor with the bent-over prongs facing out and the flat of the base plate against the feed tray. Press into the

Practical Guide to the Operational Use of the **PK / PKM Machine Gun**

feed tray and up towards the top of the cover; two small slits in the feed tray allow the restrictor to slide in. Figures 1-24a-c.

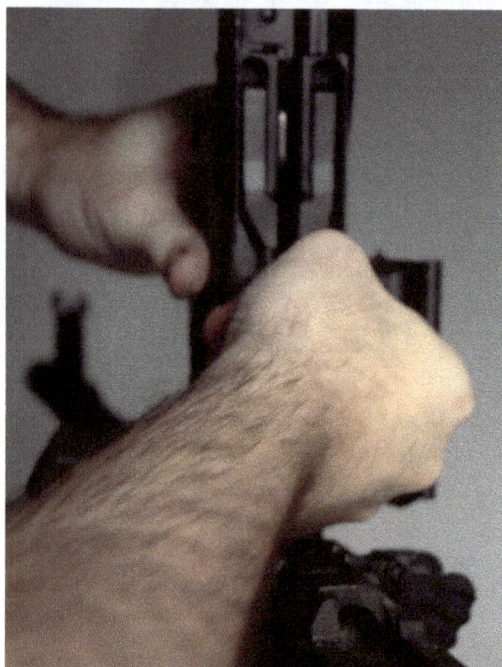
Figure 1-33a

Figure 1-33b

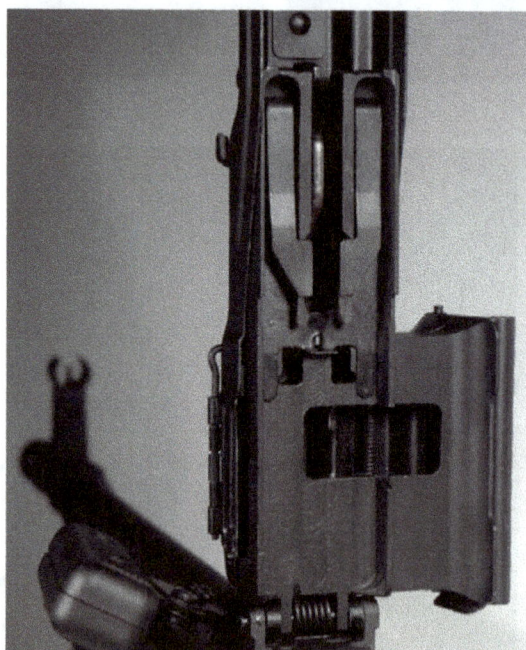
Figure 1-33c

3. The final insertion into the small slits by the base plate will require pressure in towards the feed-tray cover as this tension will hold the restrictor in place when fully seated. Note the location of the bends on the restrictor for correct placement. Figures 1-33a-c.

Figure 1-34 This photo is of the feed-tray which has been lowered. The top of the restrictor can be seen in the noted circle.

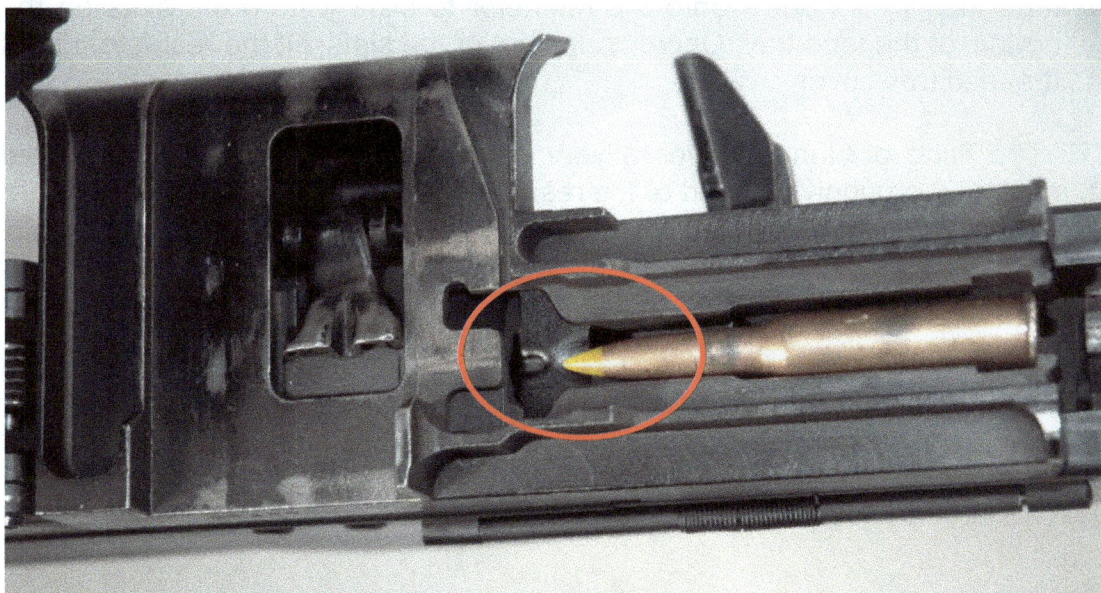

Figure 1-35 Example of what a live round would look like as it is stopped from being inserted in the chamber after it was stripped from a belt.

To remove the live round restrictor-

1. To remove the live round restrictor, ensure the weapon has been properly cleared.

Figure 1-36 Removing the live round restrictor

2. Fully open the feed-tray cover and feed tray to expose the bottom of the feed tray. Press down onto the restrictor to slide it from the slots on the bottom of the feed tray. Once it pops out of the slots, lift the restrictor out of the feed tray cover.

NOTE: The firing of blanks leaves a very corrosive agent, and all unprotected metal must be thoroughly cleaned of the residue or severe rusting will occur rather quickly, causing pitting of the metal.

Section 2

Maintenance

Clearing the PKM

Weapon condition: No ammunition belt is protruding from the right side of the receiver.

Figure 2-1 Selector in the FIRE position

1. To clear the PKM, ensure the weapon's selector is forward on FIRE. Figure 2-1.

Figure 2-2 Selector in the SAFE position

2. Pull the charging handle lever to the rear until the bolt carrier is locked to the rear by the sear, return the charging handle lever back forward, and then place the weapon on SAFE. Figure 2-2.

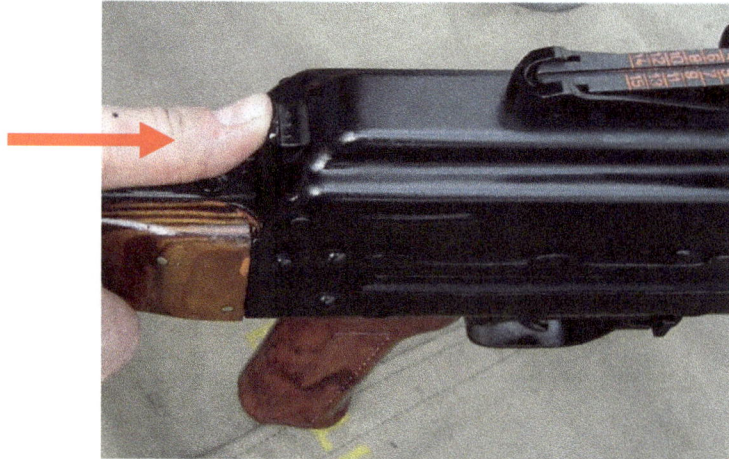

Figure 2-3 Depressing the receiver-cover latch button

3. Grasp the weapon by the skeletonized buttstock, and with your free hand, depress the receiver-cover latch button (mainspring assembly). Figure 2-3.

Figure 2-4 Raising the receiver cover

4. Raise the receiver cover to the fully open position and observe for live ammunition. Figure 2-4.

Figure 2-5 Raising the feed-tray

5. Lift the ammunition feed tray to inspect the chamber to ensure no cartridge is present. Figure 2-5.

6. Close the feed-tray cover and the receiver cover. Orient the weapon in a safe direction; place weapon on FIRE and pull the charging handle lever back and ride the bolt carrier forward by the charging handle lever. Replace the weapon's selector into the rearward SAFE position.

Clearing the loaded PKM

Weapon condition: An ammunition belt is protruding from the right side of the receiver.

Figure 2-6 Selector in the FIRE position

1. To clear the loaded PKM, the weapon's selector must be moved to the FIRE position. Figure 2-6.

2. Pull the charging handle lever to the rear to ensure the bolt carrier is locked to the rear or until it locks the bolt carrier to the rear with the sear, slide the charging handle lever back forward, and then place the weapon on SAFE.

Since the bolt carrier should be to the rear, there will be no resistance, and just the charging handle lever alone will be pulled to the rear.

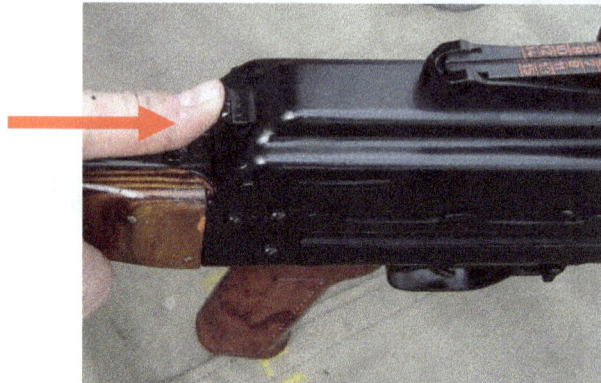

Figure 2-7 Depressing the receiver-cover latch button

3. Grasp the weapon by the skeletonized buttstock, and with your free hand, depress the receiver-cover latch button. Figure 2-7.

Figure 2-8 Raising the receiver cover

4. Raise the receiver cover to the fully open position. Once the receiver cover is fully opened, remove the ammunition belt link and the round that is on the feed tray cartridge guide. This loose round can be removed by raising the feed tray and manually removing the round from the feed tray cartridge guide.

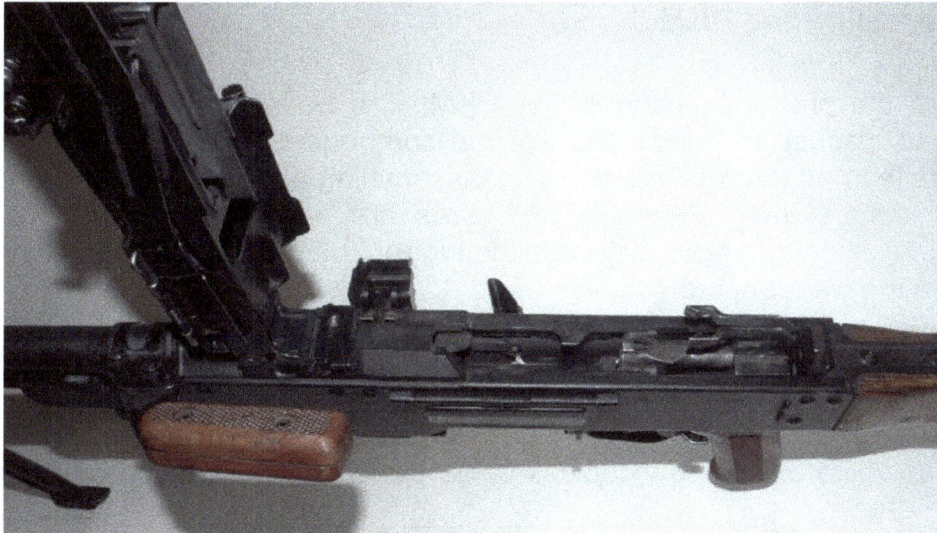

Figure 2-9 Raising the feed-tray

5. Lift the ammunition feed tray to inspect the chamber to ensure no cartridge is present.

6. Close the feed tray and the feed-tray cover. Orient the weapon in a safe direction; place weapon on FIRE and pull the charging handle lever to the rear and maintain pressure then press the trigger and ride the bolt carrier forward. Replace the weapon's selector into the rearward SAFE position.

Disassembling the PKM

To insure the proper function of the PKM, it is necessary to disassemble the weapon to inspect and clean the internal components. The names of the parts should be learned through practice in disassembling and reassembling to enhance operator competence. Generally, the parts are named for the functions they perform, i.e., the trigger guard guards the trigger, the charging handle lever is used to charge the weapon, etc.

Clear the weapon as per the above description, depending on the weapons condition.

When the operator begins to disassemble the weapon it should be done in the following order:

Figure 2-10 PKM

1. Place the weapon on a flat, clean surface with the muzzle oriented in a safe direction on the extended bipod legs or tripod. Figure 2-10.

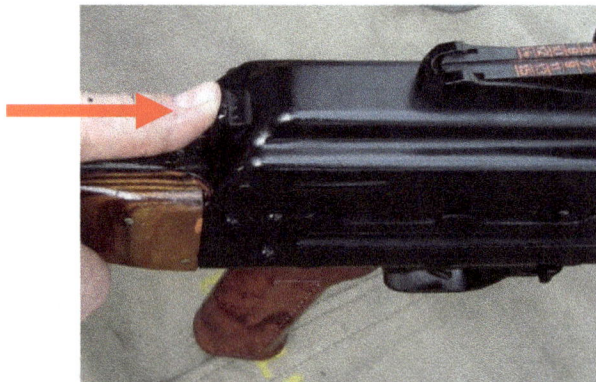

Figure 2-11 Depressing the receiver-cover latch button

2. Grasp the weapon by the skeletonized buttstock, and with your free hand, depress the receiver-cover latch button. Figure 2-11.

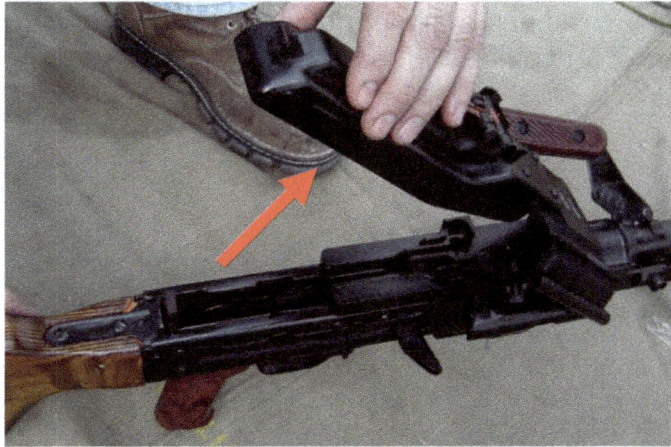

Figure 2-12 Raising the receiver cover

3. Raise the receiver cover to the fully open position. Figure 2-12.

Figure 2-13 Raising the feed-tray

4. Raise the ammunition feed-tray cover to the fully open position. Figure 2-13.

With the ammunition feed-tray cover raised, leave the cartridge gripper and bolt carrier in the forward position.

Figure 2-14a   Figure 2-14b
Removing the mainspring

5. Grasp the guide rod and mainspring while pushing forward and up to extract the mainspring and guide rod. Figures 2-14a & b.

Figure 2-15a   Figure 2-15b
Removing the bolt carrier/piston assembly

6. By holding the cartridge gripper, pull the bolt carrier and piston rod assembly to the rear and lift out, remember that the weapon's safety will need to be on FIRE to pull the bolt to the rear. Align the notches of the bolt carrier with the notches on the receiver, and then pull up on the cartridge gripper and remove the entire section from the receiver. Figures 2-15a & b.

Figure 2-16a   Figure 2-16b

Figure 2-16c Separation of bolt from bolt carrier

7. To separate the bolt and firing pin from the bolt carrier, rotate the bolt and firing pin to the rear of the carrier cam in a counter-clockwise motion. Pull

the bolt and firing pin forward while aligning the notch on the firing pin with the notch on the sliding cam. Figure 2-16a-c.

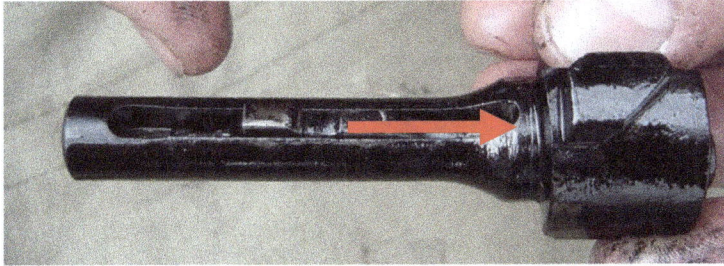

Figure 2-17a
Removing the firing pin

Figure 2-17b

8. To remove the firing pin from the bolt, push the firing pin to the rear of the bolt and rotate the bolt upside down, extracting the firing pin, or just lift it out. Figures 2-17a & b.

Figure 2-18a

Figure 2-18b
Barrel removal

Figure 2-18c

9. The next step in disassembly of the PKM is to remove the barrel. To do so, pull the barrel-locking latch completely to the left side of the receiver; the rim of a cartridge can be used. Grasp the barrel by the quick-change handle and pull the barrel forward, disengaging the barrel from the barrel-receiver group. Figures 2-18a-c.

Practical Guide to the Operational Use of the **PK / PKM Machine Gun**

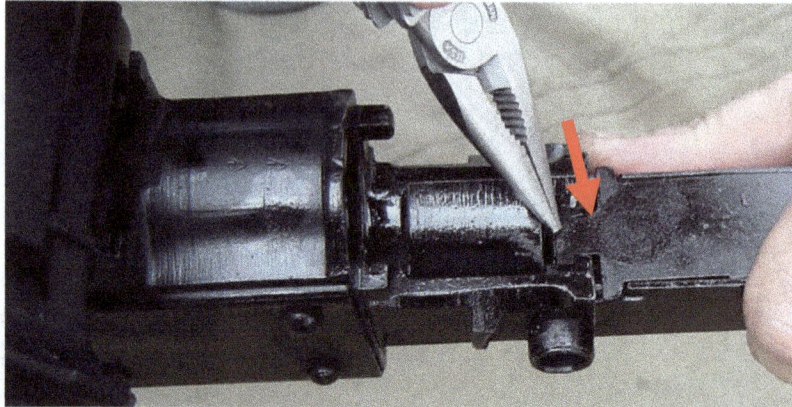

Figure 2-19 Removing the gas-piston cover

10. The final step is to remove the gas-piston cover from the receiver by pressing down on the leaf spring that is in front of the barrel receiver and sliding the gas piston cover forward from the receiver. Figure 2-19.

PKM operator level disassembled and ready for cleaning and inspection.

Figure 2-20 Disassembled PKM

1 - PKM receiver, buttstock and feed tray assembly
2 - Gas-piston cover and bipod
3 - Barrel
4 - Firing pin
5 - Bolt

6 - Bolt carrier and gas piston
7 – Operating spring and guide rod assembly

Inspecting the PKM

To insure a PKM is serviceable and ready for action, it needs to be inspected periodically and between firings. This inspection can take place while the gun team is cleaning the weapon. Disassemble as per the previous section and organize the parts in groups to be inspected.

Parts to inspect:
- The overall condition of the weapon and components.
- Individual parts-
  o The firing pin should be inspected for wear or breakage on the tip.

- o The mainspring and guide rod should be inspected to insure they have not been chipped, bent, or is broken.
- o The extractor should be checked to see that it is under spring tension and is not chipped or worn.
- o The trigger housing group should no show signs of excessive wear. All barrels should be inspected for cracks, burrs, and/or bends.
- o The gas-piston cover should be inspected to see if it has any dents that would impede the movement of the gas piston during firing.
- o The gas regulator needs to be inspected to insure it is not too covered with carbon to prevent adjustment.

Cleaning and Lubrication

The PKM is a very dependable machine gun, but periodic cleaning is advised to insure functionality. Clean the weapon as often as the situation dictates and the environment necessitates.

Keep the weapon free of dirt and dust as much as possible; use a muzzle cap or tape to keep them from the bore. Depending on the operating environment, keep lubricant only on metal-to-metal moving parts and use paint brushes to clean dust and dirt off of and out of the weapon.

Do not clean the inside of the gas-piston cover unless you have fired blanks or it is excessively sluggish induced by carbon build-up. Do not put lubricants in the gas-piston cover.

In hot and humid climates, inspect the weapon often for signs of rust. Keep the weapon free of moisture and keep a fine coat of lubricating oil on the metal surfaces. If the weapon is exposed to salt air, high humidity, or water, then clean and oil the weapon entirely as often as needed to keep serviceable.

In hot and dry climates such as deserts, keep the weapon lubricated only on metal-to-metal moving parts and use paint brushes to clean dust and dirt off of and out of the weapon. Keeping the weapon free of unneeded oil will prevent sand and dust from collecting in the receiver and bore.

Keep your ammunition in containers when not in use and clean off the links as necessary.

Clean the barrel with the cleaning rods that are stored in the bipod leg and the brushes and jags stored in the hollow section of the buttstock. Use solvent-lubricated brass brushes to break up carbon in the bore, and then use a solvent-covered patch to push the carbon out and then use a dry patch until the bore is clean. The bores are chromed lined so they clean up easily. Keep spare barrels clean by taping the chamber and muzzle, store them in the spare barrel bags and inspect regularly.

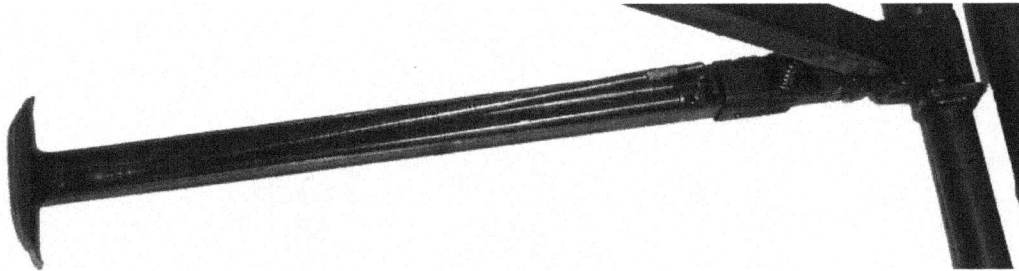

Figure 2-21 Cleaning rod storage in bipod leg

Figure 2-22 Cleaning rods removed from bipod leg

Cleaning rod sections are stored in the right side of the weapon's bipod.

Figure 2-23
Oiler in buttstock

Figure 2-24
Cleaning rod accessories storage tube

The oil well and brush are stored in the top of the buttstock, Figure 2-23. The cleaning rod accessories are kept in a steel tube fitted into the rear of the buttstock, Figure 2-24. To access this tube, you must raise the shoulder rest on the buttstock, press in the spring-loaded door and hold it open with the top of your finger to allow the tube to be spring driven out. To insert it back in, just press it in past the spring-loaded door and allow the door to close behind the tube.

Figure 2-25 Cleaning rod accessories in storage tube

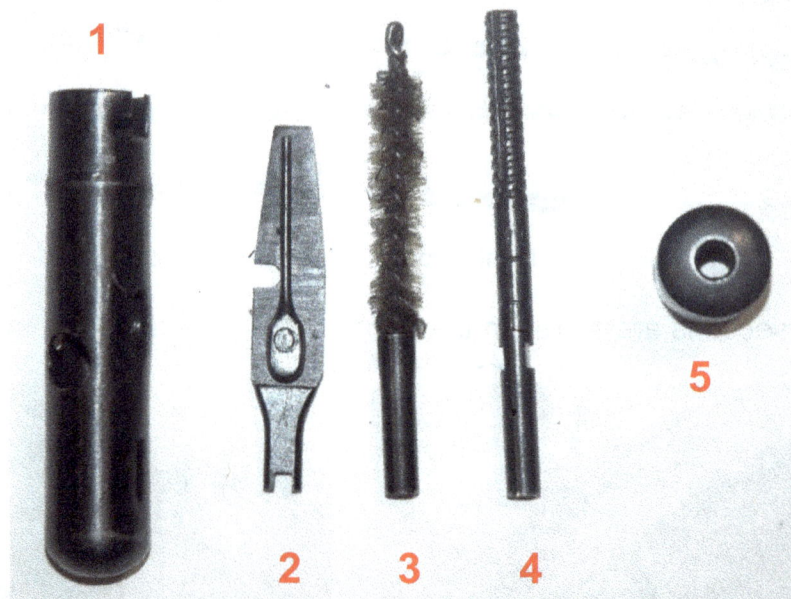

Figure 2-26 Photo of cleaning accessories in the storage tube

1- Metal storage tube - used as a handle for cleaning rod and combination tool
2- Combination tool - used to scrape carbon, as a front sight elevation tool, and punch pin for disassembling the bolt
3- Nylon bristled brush to attach to the cleaning rod sections
4- Steel patch jag to attach to the end of the cleaning rod sections
5- Metal storage tube cap - used as a cleaning rod guide

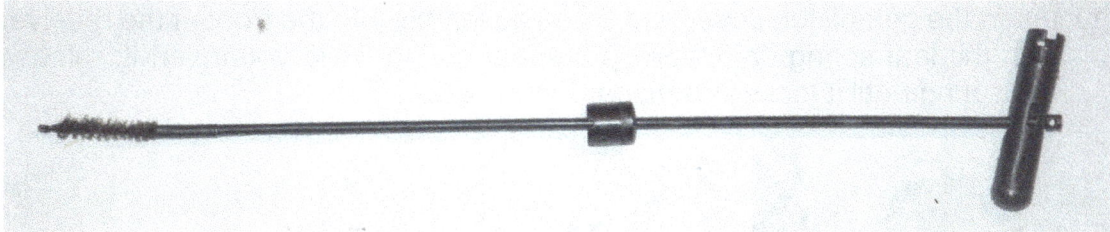

Figure 2-27 Example of the assembled rod with cap and tube used

Figure 2-28 Example of using the combo tool and tube to adjust elevation

Assembling of the PKM

As you are assembling the PKM machine gun, reinspect the internal parts to insure that each is in working order.

Figure 2-29 Attaching the gas-piston assembly

1. Insert the gas-piston cover and bipod assembly into the front of the receiver with the leaf spring up. Depress the leaf spring while you insert it; release the spring until it locks into place. Figure 2-29.

Figure 2-30a

Figure 2-30b
Installing the barrel

Figure 2-30c

2. Ensure the barrel-locking latch is fully open to the left of the receiver. Then slide the rear of the barrel into the barrel receiver group while aligning the gas escape chamber located on the front of the gas piston cover with the gas regulator on the bottom of the barrel. Figures 2-30a – c.

Figure 2-31 Locking the barrel in

3. Push the barrel locking latch to the right to lock the barrel into the receiver. Figure 2-31.

Figure 2-32
Inserting the firing pin into the bolt

4. Replace the firing pin into the bolt as shown by rotating the bolt with the long groove in the upward position. Insert the firing pin while pushing the cylindrical portion on the firing pin forward. Figure 2-32.

Figure 2-33a   Figure 2-33b
Attaching the bolt to the bolt carrier

5. Replace the rotating bolt in the sliding cam; align the notch on the firing pin with the grove on the sliding cam. Push the rotating bolt to the rear while turning the rotating bolt clockwise. Figures 2-33a & b.

Figure 2-34a   Figure 2-34b
Inserting the gas-piston assembly into the receiver

6. Insert the bolt and bolt carrier into the receiver, gas piston first. Align the notches of the bolt carrier with the grooves in the receiver. Slide the bolt carrier and piston forward while depressing the trigger. Figures 2-34a & b.

Figure 2-35a   Figure 2-35b
Inserting the mainspring assembly into the receiver

7. Insert the mainspring and guide rod; align the mainspring and guide rod with the rear opening of the sliding cam on the bolt carrier. Push the mainspring and guide rod forward and down until the notch at the end of the guide rod is seated in the receiver group. Figures 2-35a & b.

8. After the mainspring has been inserted into the receiver group, close the ammunition feed-tray cover and receiver cover.

Function Check Procedures

1. Safety Check-
    a. Pull the operating handle to the rear, and then push it forward.
    b. Rotate the safety to the rear (SAFE).
    c. Press the trigger (the bolt should no go forward).

2. Fire Check-
    a. Rotate the safety forward (FIRE).
    b. Pull the operating handle to the rear and hold it.
    c. Depress the trigger while holding the operating handle and slide the bolt forward slowly and under control.
    d. Maintain pressure on the trigger and pull the operating handle to the rear, then ease the operating handle forward (bolt should not stay to the rear).

Section 3

Operation and Function

Loading the Non-disintegrating Belt

Figure 3-1 Photo of loaded belt

Ammunition from the factory is preloaded in 25-round connectable belt lengths, Figure 3-1. To reuse the non-disintegrating belt lengths, the belt can either be loaded by hand or with the PKM mechanical belt loader. With this loader, one operator can load 25,000 per 8 hours. Figure 3-2.

Figure 3-2 Photo of belt loader

Hand loading the belt

Ensure the belts are clean, rust free, and without damage. Insert the **7.62 x 54mm R** rounds, one at a time, into each opening of the belt from the large hole to the small hole. Push the round completely forward (front edge of casing will be at the top edge of the link) into each opening. Observe basic safety precautions of handling small arms ammunition at all times. Two persons can do this quite quickly if practiced with one setting the round base down on a wooden ammo box or ammo can and the other pressing the link down onto the round. The person handling the link should wear gloves as this is quite repetitive and will quickly produce blisters. Figure 3-3.

Figure 3-3 Photo of hand loading

Improperly seated rounds will induce a failure to feed malfunction either by improper feeding of the belt or improper chambering.

Figure 3-4 Photo of 3 properly seated and 1 improperly seated live rounds in belt

Links sections are joined by mating the ends of two link sections and inserting a round. Figures 3-5a-c.

Figure 3-5a

Figure 3-5b
Joining link sections together

Figure 3-5c

Loading the PKM Machine Gun

NOTE: Keep the weapon oriented in a safe direction.

1. Clear the weapon.

Figure 3-6 Selector in FIRE position

2. Place the safety, located on the left-hand side of the weapon to the forward (fire) position. Pull the charging handle lever back and ride the bolt forward by the charging handle. Replace the weapon's selector into the rearward safe position. Figure 3-6.

Figure 3-7a   Figure 3-7b
Releasing and opening receiver cover

3. Depress the receiver cover latch, located at the rear of the upper receiver, and raise the receiver cover to the fully open position. Figures 3-7a & b.

Figure 3-8 Placing the ammunition belt

4. Place the belt to feed from right to left. It does not matter which side of the link is up as with other push-through-type feeding mechanisms as the PK/PKM cartridge gripper pulls the round from the belt and pulls it back before it rotates it to the chamber on the forward movement of the bolt carrier. The belt is then placed in the feedway, coming in from the right, with the first round gripped in the claws of the cartridge gripper. Empty casing is shown for placement into the gripper; actual ammunition would be the first round in the belt. Figure 3-8.

NOTE: the ammunition belt will not feed into the PKM from the left side of the weapon. **If the belt is loaded in this manner, you will cause damage to the feed tray cover.**

5. Close the receiver cover of the weapon, insuring that the receiver cover latch is engaged. Remember that with the weapon on safe, the bolt cannot be pulled to the rear. Figure 3-9.

Figure 3-9 Location of starter tab

For safe transport in an environment that does not require immediate action, you may use a transport mode of bolt forward with cartridge in gripper and weapon on safe or combat mode of weapon loaded and bolt back on safe, whichever the situation dictates.

Warning: When firing, if the receiver cover is not closed and the receiver cover latch is not engaged, damage to the receiver cover and injury to the operator may occur by the blow back action of the bolt and expended cartridge.

Pull the cocking handle, located on the right side of the lower receiver, completely to the rear. To extract the first round of ammunition from the belt and ready the round for firing once the trigger is depressed. Push the charging handle lever back to the forward locked position. The weapon is now ready to fire. If you are not required to fire at this time, place the selector switch back into the safe position to the rear. **Remember, the PK fires from the open bolt; pressing the trigger while riding the bolt forward will allow the weapon to fire.**

Figure 3-10 Loading the weapon with the starter tab

Another loading alternative exists when the weapon is not to be used immediately but can be quickly put into action. Have the bolt forward, feed-tray cover closed and locked, and safety selector on safe. Open the spring-loaded cover of the right side of the feed-tray cover, push the starter tab on the loaded belt through, and have the end come out of the left side under the spring-loaded link cover door. Figure 3-10.

Figure 3-11 Location of starter tab

With the starter tab correctly oriented, the turned end will allow you to hook this door with the end. Figure 3-11.

Figure 3-12a

Figure 3-12b

Figure 3-12c

Figure 3-12d

When you need to load and fire, you place the weapon on fire, pull the charging handle to the rear, and return it forward, Figures 3-12a-d,

Figure 3-13 Firing the PKM

Pull the trigger to release the bolt to go forward, repeat the charging sequence and fire the weapon. Figure 3-13.

NOTE: This method can also be used as an alternative to opening the feed-tray cover to reload a weapon that has completely fired the belt that was in the weapon. This procedure is how the M2 BMG and Mk 19 are loaded, the double cycle.

Cycle of Function

The gunners can recognize and correct stoppages when they know how the PK/PKM machine gun functions. The weapon functions automatically as long as ammunition is fed into it and the trigger is held to the rear. Each time a round is fired, the parts of the weapon function in a cycle or sequence. Many of the actions occur at the same time.

These actions are separated in this manual only for instructional purposes.

1. The cycle is started when the trigger is pulled. The trigger is pulled, releasing the sear from the sear notch. When the trigger is pulled to the rear, the rear of the sear is lowered and disengaged from the sear notch. This procedure allows the piston and bolt to be driven forward by the expansion of the operating rod spring. The cycle stops when the trigger is released and the sear again engages the sear notch on the piston.

2. The sequence of functioning is as follows:
   A. *Feeding.* As the bolt starts its forward movement, the feed pawl is forced to the right. This forces the feed-pawl over the next round in the belt, and the feed-pawl is ready to place the next round into the cartridge gripper when the rearward action occurs again. As the bolt moves to the rear after firing, the feed roller forces the feed lever to the left. This step places a round in the cartridge gripper.

B. *Chambering.* As the bolt travels forward, the upper stripping lug engages the rim of the round. The pressure of the front and rear cartridge guides holds the round so that a positive contact is made with the upper stripping lug of the bolt. The upper locking lug carries the round forward. The chambering ramp causes the nose of the round to be cammed downward into the chamber. When the round is fully seated in the chamber, the extractor snaps over the rim of the round.

C. *Locking.* As the round is chambered, the bolt enters the barrel extension. The upper and lower locking lugs contact the bolt camming surfaces on the bolt carrier and start the bolt turning clockwise. The action of the bolt into the slide assembly, as the piston continues forward, turns the bolt to complete its 90-degree (one-quarter turn) clockwise rotation. Locking is now complete.

D. *Firing.* After the bolt is fully forward and locked, the piston continues to go forward independently of the bolt for a short distance. The piston assembly carries the firing pin through the face of the bolt. The firing pin strikes the primer of the round, and the primer fires the round.

E. *Unlocking.* After the round is fired and the bullet passes the gas port, part of the expanding gases go into the gas regulator through the gas plug. The rapidly expanding gases enter into the gas cylinder from the gas regulator, forcing the piston to the rear. As the piston continues to the rear, the slide assembly's simultaneous movement to the rear causes the bolt to begin its counterclockwise rotation. The upper and lower locking lugs of the bolt contact the bolt camming surfaces of the bolt carrier and, as the bolt continues toward the rear, it completes a one-quarter turn counterclockwise. The rotation and movement to the rear unlocks the bolt from the barrel extension.

F. *Extracting.* Extracting begins during the unlocking cycle. The rotation of the bolt loosens the cartridge case in the chamber. As the piston and bolt move to the rear, the extractor pulls the cartridge case from the chamber.

G. *Ejecting.* As the cartridge case is pulled from the chamber, the bolt passes by the ejector. The extractor grips the left side of the cartridge and causes it to spin from the weapon as it reaches the ejection port. The empty non-disintegrating belt is forced out of the link ejection port as the rearward movement of the bolt causes the next round to be positioned in the feed tray.

H. *Cocking.* The piston assembly acts against the firing pin, pulling the firing pin from the primer of the spent cartridge case. The action of the piston assembly, continues to the rear with the firing pin. As long as the trigger is held to the rear, the PK/PKM will continue to complete the eight steps of functioning automatically. When the trigger is released and the sear again engages the sear notch, the cycle of functioning is stopped and the weapon is cocked. ***To prevent undue wear to the sear and sear notch, the automatic rifleman must hold the trigger firmly to the rear during firing.***

Firing the PKM

Orient toward the desired area/target, take a proper sight alignment and sight picture, rotate the selector forward to the FIRE position, and pull the trigger. You would maintain a 6-to 9-round burst for control and avoid the overheating of the barrel when possible. Firing more than 260 rounds continuously will increase the possibility of cook offs (the heat of the barrel is so great that it ignites the powder in the unchambered round).

Figure 3-14 Selector in SAFE position

Once your target engagement is complete, rotate the selector to the rear safe position. Figure 3-14.

ENGAGE TARGETS. To engage targets effectively, you will need to know how to employ the gun using the tripod, bipod, and proper body position. The non-disintegrating belt can get in the way if the gunner must move the weapon during firing.

The PKM can be fired utilizing either the attached bipod mount or by mounting the PKM on the tripod. The tripod provides the most stable base for the weapon, enabling the gunner to maximize its range capabilities and deliver a high degree of accurate fire on target.

The traversing and elevating (T&E) mechanism permits controlled manipulation in both direction and elevation and makes it possible to engage predetermined targets during darkness or periods of reduced visibility.

Trigger Manipulation

- Pull the trigger to the rear and then release. (Not squeezed, see the above cycle of function.) The weapon can be damaged by not pulling the trigger to the rear quickly and released quickly when being fired.

- Bursts of less than 6 rounds should not be fired.

- The rapid rate of fire of 200 rounds per minute is delivered in bursts of 10- to 12- rounds, which are fired 2 to 3 seconds apart.

- The sustained rate of fire of 100 rounds per minute is delivered in bursts of 6 to 8 rounds, which are fired 4 to 5 seconds apart.

Barrel Change Procedure

Changing the barrels will prolong the life of the barrel and equalize barrel wear.

| Figure 3-15a | Figure 3-15b |

Unlocking and removing the barrel

Quick change procedure –

1. Raise the feed-tray cover and push the barrel locking latch completely to the left side of the receiver. Figure 3-15a.

2. Grasp the barrel by the quick change handle and pull the barrel forward, disengaging the barrel from the barrel receiver group. Figure 3-15b.

| Figure 3-16a | Figure 3-16b |

Inserting and seating the barrel while aligning the gas block

3. To insert the new barrel, insure the barrel-locking latch is fully open to the left of the receiver. Then slide the rear of the barrel into the barrel receiver

---

group while aligning the gas escape chamber located on the front of the gas piston cover with the gas regulator on the bottom of the barrel. Figures 3-16a & b.

Figure 3-17 Locking the barrel into the receiver

4. Push the barrel-locking latch to the right to lock the barrel into the receiver. Figure 3-17.

Sights

PK/PKM Sights

The PK series machine guns (except a coaxial version PKT, which has no sights) have fully adjustable iron sights. The front sight is similar to the AK assault rifles. The post-type front has curved protective ears, and like the AK's front sight, the PKM front sight is adjustable for both windage and elevation, Figure 3-18b. The AK and PKM front sight is interchangeable. The tangent-type rear sight has an open, U-shaped notch, similar to ones used with the RPD LMG and RPK LMG, and it is adjustable for both windage and elevation, Figure 3-18a. The PKM rear sight is graduated from 100m to 1500m with 100 meter increments and 300 meter battle sight setting. The sight picture is identical to the AK assault rifles and RPK light machine guns, Figure 3-19. The scope mounting rail is located on the left side of receiver when installed.

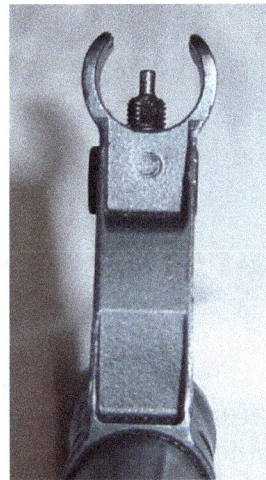

Figure 3-18a

Figure 3-18b

Photo of standard front and rear sights

Figure 3-19 Photo of standard sight alignment

Figure 3-20a
Figure 3-20b
Tritium Replacement Front Sight for PK/PKM
Item Number VSS-AK-2001-6

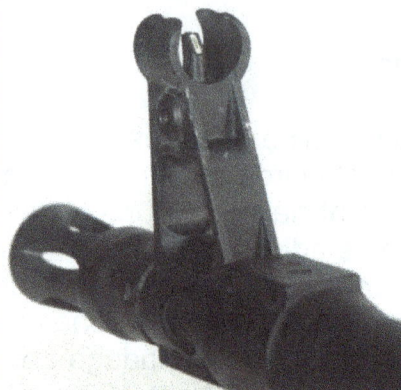

Zeroing the PKM

Zero procedure - attempt to do this on a known distance range on a windless day from a tripod.

Establish Mechanical Zero -
- Select a target between 300 and 600 meters from the weapon.
- Adjust the rear sight to the range of the target with the spring-loaded catcher; keep windage at zero
- Carefully aim and fire a 6- to 9-round burst at a paper target set up at the center of the target. If your shots are not striking the point-of-aim, then adjust your sights.
- To raise the next burst, rotate the front sight post in the down direction (clockwise). Figure 3-21b.
- To lower the next burst, rotate the front sight post in the up direction (counter-clockwise). Figure 3-21b.
- To move the next burst left, pull and turn the rear sight windage knob counterclockwise, or drift the front sight to the right.
- To move the next burst right, pull and turn the rear sight windage knob clockwise, or drift the front sight to the left.
- Continue to fire a 6- to 9-round burst and adjust the sights until you have an acceptable machine gun shot group at the point of aim. Remember, it is a machine gun and you want a beaten zone not a sniper rifle.
- Once this procedure is done, the weapon is now combat-zeroed; all other ranges on the elevation knob are also zeroed.

Figure 3-21a
Front sight being changed for the
zeroing of windage with the sight tool

Figure 3-21b
Front sight being changed for the zeroing
of elevation with the sight tool

PKM front sight adjustment, for elevation one full turn of front sight will be 4 moa and for windage using the Tapco sight tool, one full turn is 5.75 moa

PKM Bipod

The PK and its modernized version are issued with a folding bipod, which is mounted on the gas tube. The bipod's non-adjustable legs are stamped from sheet steel, and it is somewhat similar to the RPK bipod. The bipod stays automatically in its firing position by use of a spring-loaded hinge. While folded, the legs are kept together by a stamped hook. The three-piece cleaning rod is stored on the bipod right leg.

Firing from the Bipod

Figure 3-22 Firing from the bipod

The rear sight is adjusted to the desired range of target.

Assume a prone position behind the gun with the right shoulder into the weapon.

The right hand grasps the pistol grip and manipulates the trigger.

Place the left hand on the comb of the stock, palm down or up, with the cheek resting lightly against the cover and or the left hand.

Both hands apply a firm steady pressure to the rear during aiming and firing.

The bipod is not stable like tripod; the body may move.

When changing direction for minor adjustments, shift the shoulders and torso slightly.

When changing direction for major adjustments, the entire body must be moved.

Changing elevation is done by moving the elbows further apart or closer together.

Bipod Firing Positions -

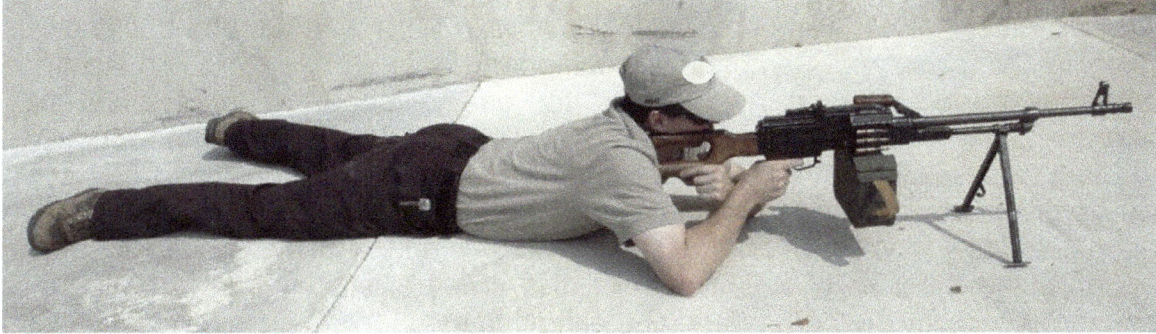

Figure 3-23 Prone bipod position

Figure 3-24 Standing bipod position

PKM Stepanova Tripod

The PK machine gun was originally introduced in 1961 with a tripod designed by Evgeniy Samozhenkov. Samozhenkov's tripod weighed 7.7 kg/17 lbs., almost half less than the SGM tripod, and it converted easily to both ground fire and anti-aircraft configurations. When the improved the PKM pattern was introduced in 1969, it was issued with a new and remarkably lighter tripod designed by Leonid Stepanova. The Stepanova mount can easily be described as a "light" tripod. Made almost entirely from steel stampings, it weighs only 4.5 kg/10 lbs. It has no buffering mechanism of any sort, and the cradle, which mounts the gun, is connected directly on the traverse and elevation mechanism. The Stepanova light tripod can be easily modified from ground fire role to an anti-aircraft configuration.

Each tripod leg can be folded for transport or adjusted for proper height or finding equilibrium in rugged terrain. While folded for transport, the tripod can be easily carried in the field by one man. Like any other tripod, the Stepanova light tripod requires sandbags for maximum stability.

The Stepanova tripod issued with our test gun was manufactured in Kovrov (marked with an arrow inside oval ring) in 1977. It appeared to be unused. The tripod was clean and dry, apparently stored 20 years ago by wrapping it in paper treated with corrosion-inhibiting agent and putting it in a sealed container. During these years, all lubricant had dried and frozen most moving parts. It required some muscle and lot of gun oil to get all hinged parts operating properly. Please note: If you are handling wrappings etc., treated with Soviet/Warsaw Pact corrosion-inhibiting agent, bear in mind that it is very poisonous.

T&E - The traversing and elevation mechanism (T&E) provides controlled manipulation of the weapon and the ability to engage predetermined targets in times of low visibility.

Tripod Employment

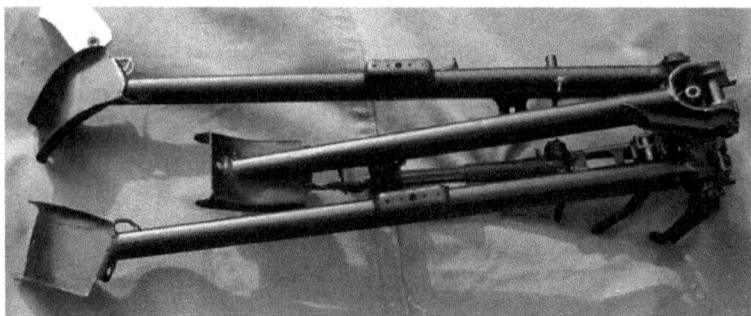
Figure 3-25 Tripod folded for storage/transport

Configuring the tripod for ground use from the collapsed carry position, Figure 3-25 - Always store your tripod in the carry bag to keep it free from mud, dirt, and dust.

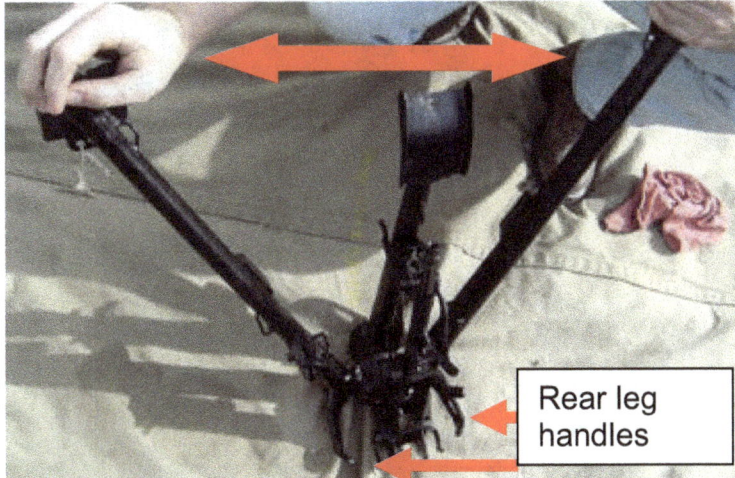

Figure 3-26 Opening the rear legs

1. Unlock rear leg handles and separate the rear legs outward. Tighten the handles once the legs are at the desired position. Figure 3-26.

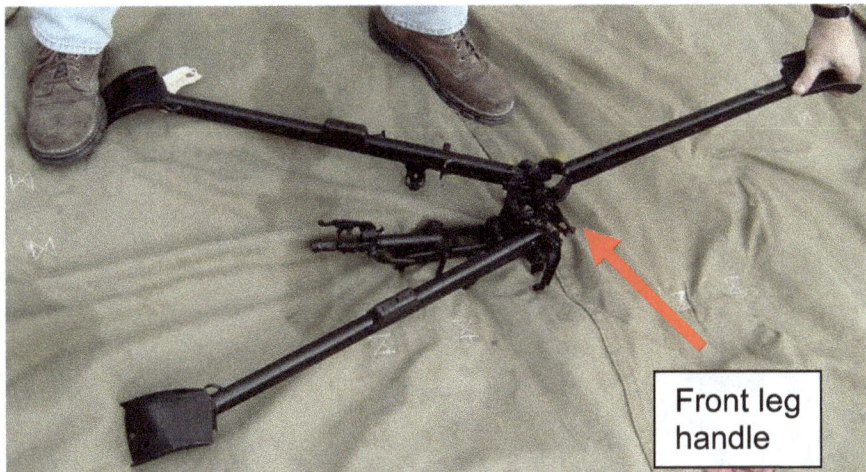

Figure 3-27 Extending the front leg

2. Lay the tripod onto its pintle, unlock the front leg handle, and swivel the front leg down away from the rear legs (you may have to stand on the rear leg to hold the tripod). Tighten the handle once the front leg is at the desired position. Figure 3-27.

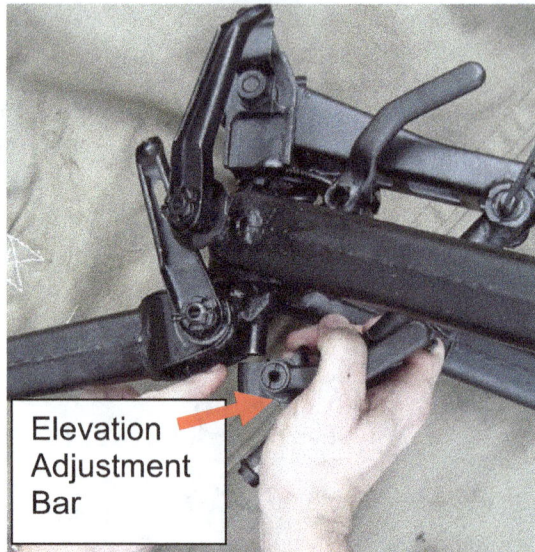

Figure 3-28 Attaching the elevation adjustment bar

3. Lay the tripod on its side and rotate the elevation adjustment bar under the pintle and lock it onto the stud. Figure 3-28.

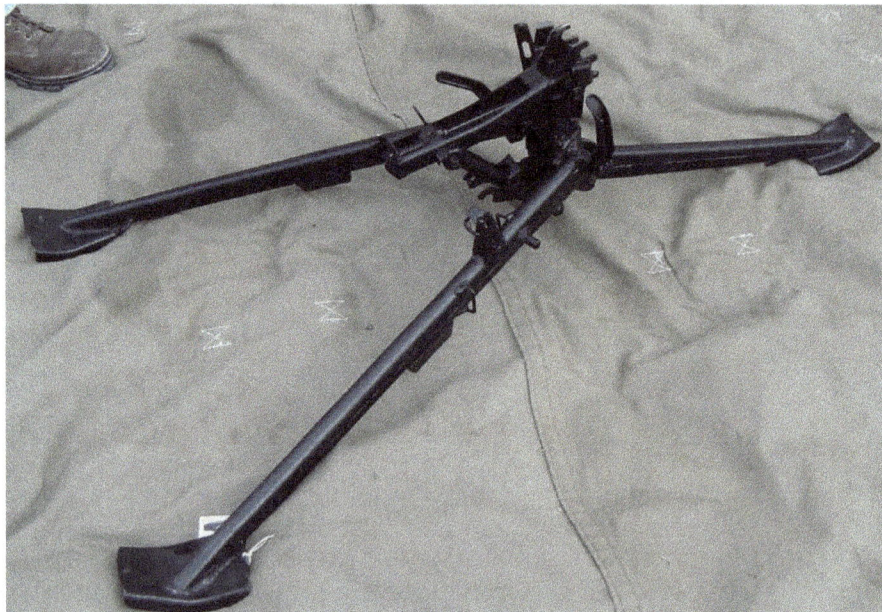

Figure 3-29 Tripod prepared for mounting the PKM

4. Tripod is now prepared for the mounting of the gun. To change the height and angle of the tripod legs just loosen the desired leg's handle, move to desired position and retighten the handle. This is one of the lightest and most versatile and adaptable tripods in the world. Figure 3-29.

Mounting the PK onto the Tripod

Figure 3-30 Inserting the receiver lugs into the pintle slots

1. Place the lugs on the bottom front of the receiver into the mating slots on the front of the tripod pintle. Figure 3-30.

Figure 3-31a   Figure 3-31b
Seating and locking in the rear of the receiver

2. While pulling the weapon to the rear to keep the lugs in the tripod slots, rotate the butt of the weapon down. Once the weapon is down onto the rear of the pintle, press the pintle lock down lever forward and finish lowering the weapon onto the pintle. Now you can let go of the pintle lock down lever, and the weapon is locked onto the tripod. For stability, the legs may need to be dug in or have sandbags placed on them, depending how long you will occupy your position and angles of firing. Figures 3-31a & b.

Figure 3-32 Tripod mounted PKM

Figure 3-33 Attaching the ammunition can to the tripod leg

Attaching the ammunition can to the tripod - On the right rear leg of the tripod is an attachment point. Open the latch, place the can tab on the point, and lock the latch back. Figure 3-33.

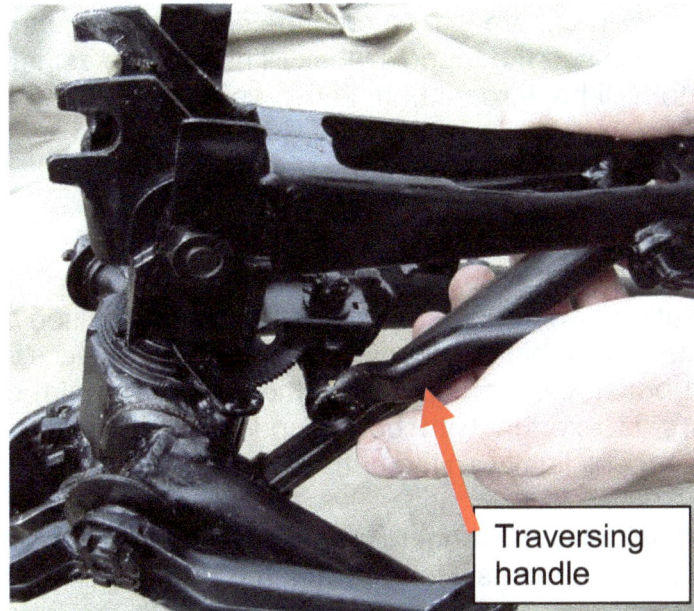

Figure 3-34 Opening the rear legs

Adjusting and locking in traversing adjustments - Loosen the handle, move the weapon left or right, and retighten handle. Figure 3-34.

Figure 3-35a
PKM and tripod in AA mode

Figure 3-35b
Unlocking the elevation adjustment bar

Once the tripod is configured for ground use, it can quickly and easily be transformed for anti-aircraft or high-angle fire. With the weapon off the tripod, unlock the elevation adjustment bar and swivel it up to a vertical position, Figure

3-35b. Now the weapon can be locked onto the elevation adjustment bar for high-angle firing; as you can see the tripod's legs will need to be adjusted to stand taller so that the operator will have room behind the weapon. Figure 3-35a.

Proper Body Position to Fire

The Gunner's Position - The gunner assumes the prone position behind the gun in the same manner as with a bipod-mounted gun. The difference is with the left hand. The skeletonized buttstock is grasped with the left hand, palm down, and a firm rearward pressure is exerted with both hands. Exert pressure with the right shoulder. Rest the cheek lightly on the butt stock of the gun while aiming and firing.

The Team Leader's/Assistant Gunner Position - This position is the same for both bipod- and tripod-mounted guns. He assumes a prone position on the right side of the gun, ensuring that his head and eyes are even with the feed way. He loads, unloads, and changes barrels from this position.

Firing

Point the muzzle of the gun in the general direction of the target by releasing the traversing lock. Secure the lock lever when on target.

Place the estimated range on the rear sight, and manipulate the gun until there is a proper sight picture.

Unlike the bipod, the tripod provides a stable base and controlled manipulation, making the use of the sight redundant.

Manipulation - All manipulation is accomplished by loosening the two hand levers with the left hand. If both direction and elevation changes are required to engage a target, manipulate direction first, then elevation.

To traverse, place the left hand on the traversing hand lever, thumb up. To move the muzzle to the right, the gunner pushes away with the thumb: PUSH RIGHT. To move the muzzle to the left, the gunner pulls to the rear with the thumb: PULL LEFT.

To search, rest the left hand on the elevating hand lever. To move the muzzle up, the gunner pushes away with the thumb: PUSH UP. To move the muzzle down, the gunner pulls to the rear with the thumb: PULL DOWN

Other PKMS firing positions

Figure 3-36 Prone tripod position

Figure 3-37 Seated tripod position

Figure 3-38 Anti-aircraft/High-angle tripod position

Vehicle Mount

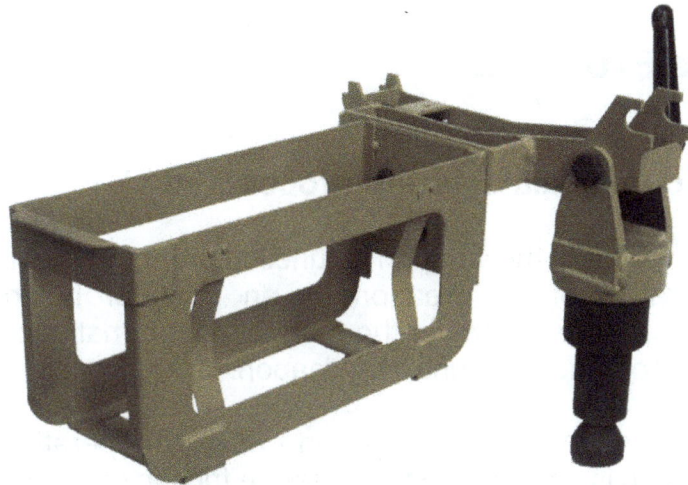

Figure 3-39 PKM vehicle mount

PKM Vehicle Mount- This mount is a custom-made high-quality mount to allow the operator to mount a PKM to all US military pintle mounts, whether a US tripod, ring mount, or pedestal mount that is also available.

In addition to the mounts described above, there exists a flexible vehicle mount, which accepts a standard PK or PKM.

Section 4

Performance Problems

Malfunction and Immediate Action Procedures-

A malfunction is a failure of the weapon to function properly. Defective ammunition or improper operation of the weapon by an operator is not considered a malfunction of the weapon. Some of the more common malfunctions of the PKM are sluggish operation and or a runaway weapon.

Sluggish operation and the corrective action - Sluggish operation (Gun fires very slowly) of the weapon is usually due to excessive friction caused by dirt or carbon, lack of proper lubrication, burred parts, or excessive loss of gas. Move the gas regulator setting to the number two or three position and re-test until the weapon functions properly. If this step does not correct the sluggish operation, then disassemble, clean, and lubricate the weapon while inspecting the parts for burrs or damage. Replace parts as necessary.

Figure 4-1   Figure 4-1b   Figure 4-1c
Using a casing to adjust the gas setting

Gas regulator settings 1, 2, and 3; use the base of a cartridge to aid in the adjusting. Figures 4-1a-c.

Runaway weapon and corrective action - A runaway weapon is a weapon that continues to fire after the trigger has been released. It may be induced by a worn sear, worn sear notch, or short recoil, i.e., the operating group recoils to feed and fire but not sufficiently enough for the sear to engage the sear notch. Short recoil may be caused by loss of gas or excessive carbon buildup in the operating rod tube. To correct this condition, hold the weapon on target until the ammunition belt is expended. Disassemble the weapon and check the gas port plug, and gas cylinder extension and clean the operating rod. Replace parts as necessary and re-test.

Stoppages - A stoppage is an interruption in the cycle of operation caused by a faulty gun or ammunition. In short, the gun stops firing. A stoppage must be cleared quickly by applying immediate action.

Immediate Action - This is the prompt action taken by the gunner to reduce a stoppage of the machine gun without investigating the cause. If the gun stops firing, the gunner performs immediate action. Hang fire and cook off are two terms that describe ammunition condition and should be understood in conjunction with immediate action procedures.

Hang Fire - Occurs when the cartridge primer has detonated after being struck by the firing pin, but some problem with the propellant powder causes it to burn too slowly, and this delays the firing of the projectile. Time (5 seconds) is allotted for this malfunction before investigating a stoppage further because of potential injury to personnel and damage to equipment.

Cook Off - Occurs when the heat of the weapon is high enough to cause the propellant powder inside the round to ignite even though the primer has not been struck. Immediate action is to unload the weapon immediately and allow it cool prior to reloading and firing.

Misfire Procedures

Immediate action - This action is performed when the operator has a failure to fire, which is when the trigger is pulled, the bolt moves forward, and the weapon does not fire. If a cartridge case, belt link, or a round is ejected, push the charging handle lever to its forward position, take aim on the target, and pull the trigger. If the weapon does not fire, take remedial action. If a cartridge case, belt link, or a round is not ejected, take remedial action.

Remedial Action - When immediate action fails to reduce the stoppage, remedial action must be taken. Prior to investigating the cause of the stoppage, you must clear the weapon, and this step may involve some disassembly of the weapon and replacement of parts to correct the problem. Remedial actions for stoppages are as follows.

Stuck Cartridge - Some swelling of the cartridge occurs when it fires. If the swelling is excessive, the cartridge will be fixed tightly in the chamber. If the extractor spring has weakened and does not tightly grip the base of the cartridge, it may fail to extract a round when the bolt moves to the rear.

1. Ensure the bolt is locked to the rear.
2. Place the weapon on safe and allow the gun to cool if it is a hot gun.
3. Insert a length of cleaning rod into the muzzle to push the round out through the chamber.

WARNING: If nothing is ejected and the barrel is hot (200 rounds or more in 2 minutes or less), do not open the cover. Push the safety to the rear, which places the weapon on safe. Keep the weapon pointed down range and remain clear for 15 minutes, and then clear the weapon.

Ruptured Cartridge - Sometimes a cartridge is in a weakened condition after firing. In addition, it may swell as described above. In this case, a properly functioning extractor may sometimes tear the base of the cartridge off as the bolt moves to the rear, leaving the rest of the cartridge wedged inside the chamber. The ruptured cartridge extractor must be used in this instance to remove it.

Remove the barrel and insert the shell extractor into the chamber to grip and remove the remains of the cartridge.

Figure 4-2 Photo of cartridge extractor

The ruptured case extractor must be used if the empty cartridge case is ripped in half leaving the front half of the casing in the chamber preventing the next loaded round to seat in to the chamber. To extract this case neck, you must screw the extractor on the rod section and push it up into the chamber fully so you can pull the case neck out. Figure 4-2.

Appendix A - Ammunition Comparison

9x18mm Makarov

9x19mm Luger

7.62x25mm Tokarev

.45 ACP

PISTOLS AND SUBMACHINE GUNS

Size Comparison of NATO vs. Non-Standard Ammunition

5.56x 45mm

5.45x 39mm

5.56x 45mm

7.62x 39mm

7.62x 51mm

7.62x 54R mm

12.7x 99mm

12.7x 108mm

ASSAULT RIFLES

SNIPER RIFLES & MACHINE GUNS

Appendix B - Non-Standard Ammunition Packaging & Markings

Packaging

Russian small arms cartridges are packed in sealed sheet-metal containers, with two containers per wooden crate. Older Russian production used rectangular containers of heavy gauge galvanized iron with soldered seams. Around 1959, the introduction of painted, rolled edge, rounded corner, tin plate 'sardine can' containers became the standard.

Metal and wooden crates have standardized markings that identify the contents as to caliber, functional type, cartridge case material, quantity and cartridge/powder lot data. Specialized cartridges are further identified by a color code consisting of one or two color stripes which correspond to bullet tip color. AP cartridges with tungsten carbide cores are identified by two concentric circles instead of color stripes. Russian cartridge designation, packaging and marking practices are generally followed by former Soviet-Bloc countries; each, however, has introduced some modifications in designation and marking. Russian ammunition packaging can be distinguished from Bulgarian packaging, which also carries Cyrillic markings, primarily by the different factory codes. The factory code on the container also appears in the headstamp of the cartridges in the container.

Steel Ammo Tins
(Sardine Cans)

Wood Ammo Crate (Case)
(Contains 2 Tins + Opener)

Cartridge quantities and weights of wooden crates

Country	Manufacturer	Caliber	Rounds /Crate	Crate Weight
Czech Rep.	Sellier and Bellot	14.5 x 114	210	53 kg.
India	OFB	14.5 x 114	60	15.5 kg.
Russia	Unknown	14.5 x 114	80	23 kg.
Bulgaria	Arsenal	12.7 x 108	200	29 kg.
Bulgaria	Arsenal	12.7 x 108	200	32 kg.
Pakistan	POF	12.7 x 108	280	42 kg.
Russia	Unknown	12.7 x 108	190	29 kg.
Russia	Novosibirsk	12.7 x 108	160	25 kg.
Bulgaria	Arsenal	7.62 x 54(R)	880	25 kg.
Czech Rep.	Sellier and Bellot	7.62 x 54(R)	800	24 kg.
Russia	Novosibirsk	7.62 x 54(R)	880	26 kg.
Russia	Novosibirsk	7.62 x 54(R)	600	21 kg.
Russia	Unknown	7.62 x 54(R)	880	26 kg.
Serbia	Prvi Partizan	7.62 x 54(R)	1,200	39 kg.
Czech Rep.	Sellier and Bellot	7.62 x 39	1,200	28 kg.
Pakistan	POF	7.62 x 39	1,750	39 kg.
Russia	Barnaul	7.62 x 39	1,320	30 kg.
Serbia	Prvi Partizan	7.62 x 39	1,260	29 kg.
Sudan	STC	7.62 x 39	1,500	28.1 kg.
Ukraine	Lugansk	7.62 x 39	1,320	30 kg.
Yugoslavia	Igman Zavod	7.62 x 39	1,260	28 kg.
Yugoslavia	Igman Zavod	7.62 x 39	1,120	27.5 kg.
Russia	Unknown	5.45 x 39	2,160	29 kg.
Ukraine	Lugansk	5.45 x 39	2,160	29 kg.

Non-Standard Ammunition tin and crate marking - diagrams

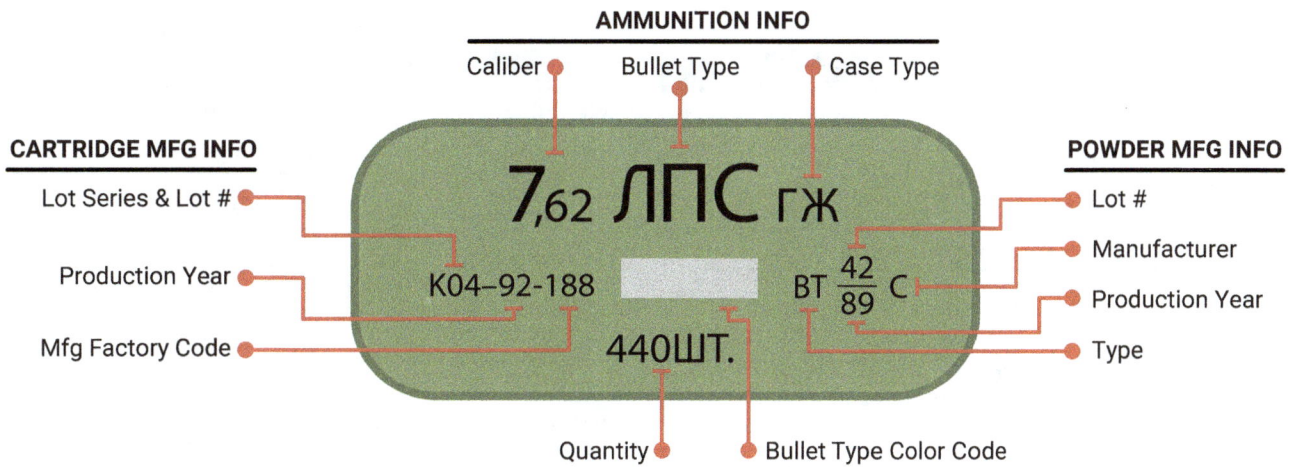

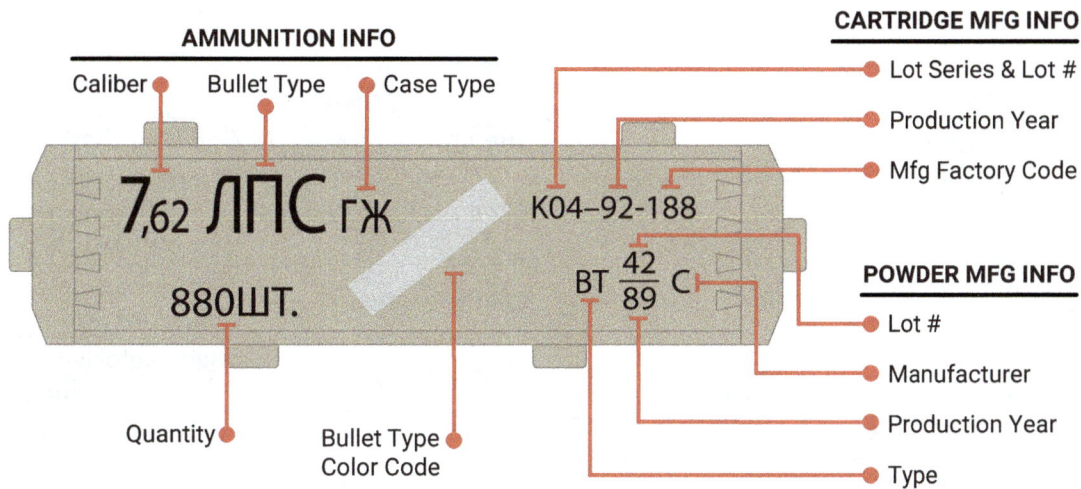

AMMUNITION INFO

Caliber   Bullet Type   Case Type

CARTRIDGE MFG INFO

Lot Series & Lot #

Production Year

Mfg Factory Code

7,62 ЛПС ГЖ

K04–92–188

440ШТ.

BT $\frac{42}{89}$ C

POWDER MFG INFO

Lot #

Manufacturer

Production Year

Type

Quantity   Bullet Type Color Code

AMMUNITION INFO

Caliber   Bullet Type   Case Type

7,62 ЛПС ГЖ

880ШТ.

K04–92–188

BT $\frac{42}{89}$ C

CARTRIDGE MFG INFO

Lot Series & Lot #

Production Year

Mfg Factory Code

POWDER MFG INFO

Lot #

Manufacturer

Production Year

Type

Quantity   Bullet Type Color Code

Non-Standard Ammunition tin and crate marking - Russian ammunition data

CASE TYPE MARKINGS

Mark	Meaning
ГЖ	Bimetallic case (gilding metal clad steel)
ГЛ	Brass case
ГС	Steel case

CARTRIDGE MFG FACTORY CODES

Code	Location
3	Ulyanovsk
17	Barnaul
38	Yuryuzan
60	Frunze (now Bishkek)
188	Novosibirsk
270	Voroshilovgrad (now Luhansk)
304	Lugansk
539	Tula
711	Klimovsk
T	Tula

Non-Standard Ammunition tin and crate marking - Russian ammunition data

BULLET TYPE MARKINGS

Mark	Meaning
Б Б-30 Б-32 БП	Armor-piercing
БЗ	Armor-piercing incendiary
БЗТ БЗТ-44	Armor-piercing incendiary tracer
БС БС-40 БС-41	Armor-piercing with special core of tungsten carbide instead of carbon steel
БСТ	Armor-piercing with tungsten carbide core with added tracer
БТ	Armor-piercing tracer
Д	Heavy (long-range) with lead core instead of carbon steel
З ЗП	Incendiary
Л	Lightweight bullet
ЛПС	Light ball bullet with mild steel core
МДЗ	High explosive incendiary
П П-41	Spotting / ranging
ПЗ	Incendiary spotting / ranging
ПП	Enhanced penetration
ПС	Spotting / ranging with mild steel core
ПТ	Spotting / ranging tracer
СНБ	Armor-piercing sniper
Т Т-30 Т-45 Т-46	Tracer
57-У-322 57-У-323	Cartridge with higher powder charge
57-У-423	High-pressure cartridge
57-Х-322 57-Х-323 57-Х-340	Blank cartridge
57-НЕ-УЧ	Training cartridge
7Н1	Sniper bullet

BULLET TYPE COLOR CODES (Ammunition up to 14.5mm)

Color	Meaning
No color	Ball
White tip	Reference Ball
Silver tip	Light ball with steel core
Yellow tip	Heavy ball, or ball with torpedo base (on 7.62x54R)
Blue tip + white band	Short range ball 14.5x114 (only Hungarian and Czech)
Green tip + white band	Short range, tracer, (only Czech designation, only found on 7.62x39 with round nose)
Green tip	Tracer
Green tip & head-stamp or entire cartridge green	Subsonic ammunition for silencer-weapons
Red tip	Spotting charge, incendiary
Red tip + white band	Short range tracer ball 14.5x114 (only Hungarian designation)
Entire bullet red	High explosive bullet (7.62x54R after 1945)
Entire bullet red	High explosive bullet (on 12.7 and 14.5mm)
Magenta tip + red band	Armor piercing incendiary tracer
Black tip + red band	Armor piercing incendiary
Black tip + red shell	Armor piercing incendiary with tungsten carbide core
Black tip + yellow band	Armor piercing incendiary Phosphorus 12.7
Black tip	Armor piercing

** The bullet tip color codes in the table above will be the same color codes on the tins or crates, but they will be color stripes on the packaging.

Example:

CARTRIDGE
Black Tip + Red Band

TIN or CRATE
Black Stripe + Red Stripe

Appendix C - Non-Standard Weapon Identification Markings

General Identification Markings

There are various identification markings found on non-standard weapons. Typically the markings will provide some or all of the following information:

- factory name or stamp (proof mark)
- caliber & serial number
- selector lever markings/symbols
- rear sight mark/symbol

NOTE: Data tables are not all inclusive, but they cover the more common weapon manufacturers.

Selector Lever Markings on Kalashnikov Rifles

Upper/ Safe Symbol	Mid/ Full-Auto Symbol	Lower/ Semi-Auto Symbol	Country
	Д	1	Albania
	L	D	Albania
	АВ	ЕД	Bulgaria
	L	D	China
	连	单	China
	30	1	Czechoslovakia
	آلى	فردى	Egypt
	D	E	Egypt
	D	E	East Germany
	∞	1	Hungary
أ	ص	م	Iraq
	련	단	North Korea
	C	P	Poland
	Z	O	Poland
S	A	R	Romania
S	FA	FF	Romania
	1	3	Romania
	ЛР	ОГОНЬ	Russia
	АВ	ОД	Russia
U	R	J	Yugo/Serbia

Rear Sight Marks on Kalashnikov Rifles

Symbol	Country
D	Albania
П	Bulgaria
D	China
N	East Germany
A	Hungary
ㅍ	North Korea
S	Poland
P	Romania
П	Russia
O	Yugo/Serbia

DShK Selector Markings

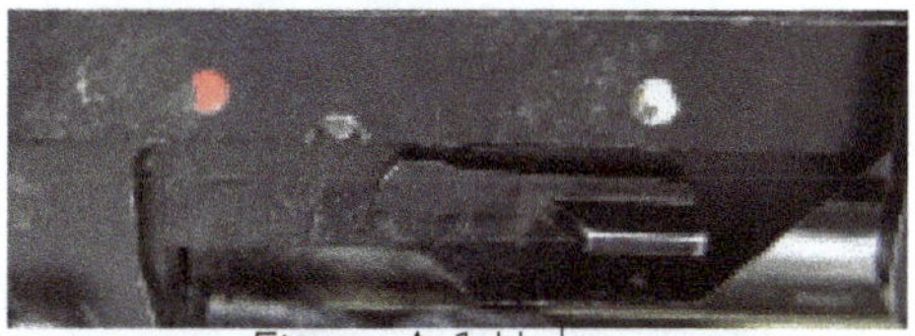

Figure A-1 Unknown
RED = FIRE WHITE = SAFE

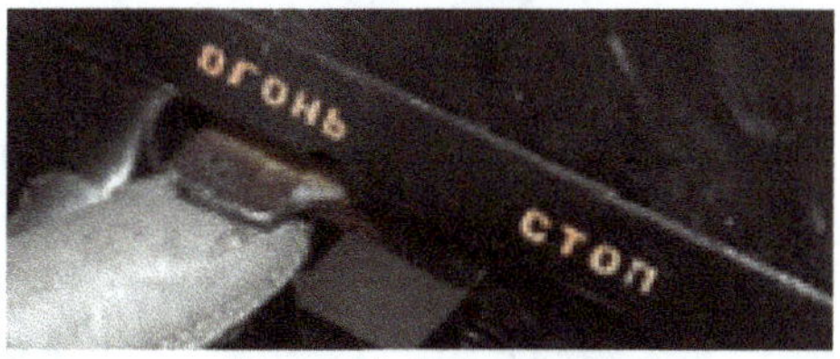

Figure A-2 Russian
Огонь translates to FIRE
Стоп translates to STOP

Non-Standard Weapon Identification Markings

Factory Stamps and Countries of Manufacture

The table of symbols below are factory stamps (proof marks) for non-standard weapons. The symbols will identify the country of manufacture of the weapon. NOTE: *This is not an all inclusive list, but it covers the more common weapon manufacturers.*

Bulgaria	Bulgaria	Bulgaria	China
China	China	China	China
Egypt	East Germany	East Germany	East Germany
East Germany	East Germany	Iraq	Iraq
North Korea	North Korea	Poland	Romania
Russia	Russia	Russia	Russia
Russia	Russia	Russia	Russia
Yugoslavia/Serbia	Yugoslavia/Serbia	Yugoslavia/Serbia	

M.70.AB2   ZASTAVA-KRAGUJEVAC

Appendix D - Non-standard weapons theory overview

There are three key concepts to understand when manipulating non-standard weapons. These simple and logical concepts are:

1. CYCLE OF OPERATIONS
2. OPERATING SYSTEMS
3. LOCKING SYSTEMS

> Firearm design trends are shared across region, manufacturer and class of weapon and are relatively obvious to recognize.
>
> Keep in mind that firearms are essentially simple machines that harness the energy created by the fired cartridge to operate the system.

CYCLE OF OPERATIONS (COO)

The cycle of operations is a crucial basis for understanding how the weapon operates and for function/malfunction diagnosis. Each specific malfunction will correspond to a specific step or sometimes two in the COO. A failure in the system at a certain point, will by default, cause a failure of omission of all subsequent steps. (example – a failure to properly extract will manifest as a failure to eject.)

The COO will vary based on the type of operating and locking systems. Once the operating and locking systems of the weapon are known, the COO is logical.

The examples below all start from a standard reference point: the weapon is loaded, charged, placed on fire and the trigger is pulled.

'Cycle of Operations' Examples:

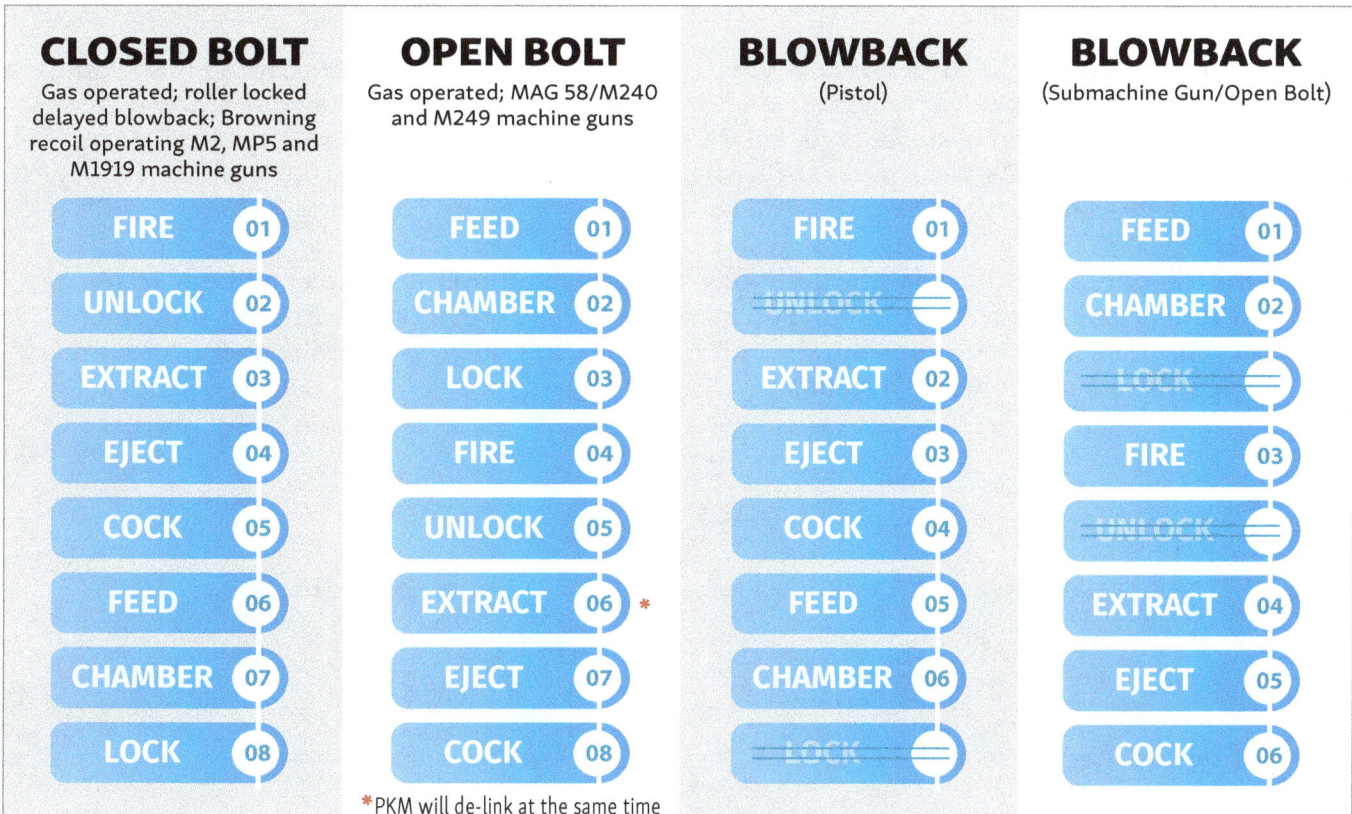

CLOSED BOLT
Gas operated; roller locked delayed blowback; Browning recoil operating M2, MP5 and M1919 machine guns

01	FIRE
02	UNLOCK
03	EXTRACT
04	EJECT
05	COCK
06	FEED
07	CHAMBER
08	LOCK

OPEN BOLT
Gas operated; MAG 58/M240 and M249 machine guns

01	FEED
02	CHAMBER
03	LOCK
04	FIRE
05	UNLOCK
06	EXTRACT *
07	EJECT
08	COCK

*PKM will de-link at the same time

BLOWBACK
(Pistol)

01	FIRE
~~UNLOCK~~	~~UNLOCK~~
02	EXTRACT
03	EJECT
04	COCK
05	FEED
06	CHAMBER
~~LOCK~~	~~LOCK~~

BLOWBACK
(Submachine Gun/Open Bolt)

01	FEED
02	CHAMBER
~~LOCK~~	~~LOCK~~
03	FIRE
~~UNLOCK~~	~~UNLOCK~~
04	EXTRACT
05	EJECT
06	COCK

Non-standard weapons theory overview *(continued ...)*

⚙ <u>**OPERATING SYSTEMS**</u>

1. **Direct Impingement**- a type of gas operation that directs gas from a fired cartridge directly to the bolt carrier or slide assembly to cycle the action. (AR-15/M4 variants)

2. **Long-stroke piston system**- the piston is mechanically fixed to the bolt group and moves through the entire operating cycle. (AK variants)

3. **Short-stroke piston system (tappet system)**- the piston moves separately from the bolt group. It may directly push the bolt group parts as n the M1 carbine or operate through a connecting rod. (HK 416, AR180, POF, LWRC, FN FAL)

4. **Blowback**- the system of operation for self-loading firearms that obtains energy from the motion of the cartridge case as it is pushed to the rear by expanding gases created by the ignition of the propellant charge. (STEN, Makarov, M3 Grease Gun)

5. **Short recoil action**- the barrel and slide recoil only a short distance before they unlock and separate. The barrel stops quickly, and the slide continues rearward compressing the recoil spring and performing extraction, ejection and finally feeding a fresh round from the magazine in the counter recoil phase. During the last portion of its forward travel, the slide locks into the barrel and pushes the barrel back into battery. *(This is found in most handguns chambered for 9x19mm Parabellum or greater caliber. Smaller calibers, 9x18mm Makarov and below, generally use the blowback method of operation due to lower chamber pressure and associated simplicity of design.)

6. **Roller-locked, delayed-blowback**- when the bolt is closed, the rollers carried in the bolt are wedged into the receiver recesses. On firing, the rollers must be forced out of the recesses at great mechanical disadvantage, delaying the opening of the bolt, even with full power 7.62mm NATO (.308 Winchester) rifle cartridges used in the G3/HK 91 (G3, HK 91, HK 93, HK 53, MP5 variants)

7. **Inertia operated systems**- the bolt body is separated from the locked bolt body to remain stationary while the recoiling gun and locked bolt head moves rearward. This movement compresses the spring between the bolt head and bolt body, storing the energy required to cycle the action. Benelli shotguns.

Non-standard weapons theory overview *(continued ...)*

🔒 **LOCKING SYSTEMS**

1. **None** - all blowback pistols and some submachine guns – (STEN, UZI, M3 Grease Gun, Makarov, and CZ 82)

2. **Roller** - (HK variants, MG3, MG34, MG 42 and CZ 52)

3. **Rotating bolt** - (AK, Stoner, M60, and M249)

4. **Tilting bolt** - (SKS, FN FAL and MAG 58/M240)

5. **Tilting barrel** - (Tokarev TT33, Sig variants, M1911 variants and Glock variants)

6. **Rotating barrel** - (MAB P15, Colt All American 2000, and Beretta 8000)

7. **Locking flaps** - (RPD, DP/DPM and DShK)

8. **Falling locking block** - (P38, M9, and VZ58)

Function check
Checking the mechanical function of a weapon by replicating, without ammunition, the firing modes from the lowest rate of fire (SAFE if applicable) to the highest in a progressive sequence (not by selector location). The parts checked are the safety/safeties, sear and disconnector.

M4A1
1. Ensure the rifle is clear
2. Charge and place the weapon on SAFE
3. Attempt to fire (weapons should not FIRE, safety is functioning)
4. Place the weapon on SEMI, pull the trigger and hold it to the rear (hammer should fall, trigger/sear functioning)
5. Maintain the trigger to the rear and cycle the bolt
6. Release the trigger and listen for a metallic click (disconnector functioning)
7. Pull the trigger again and the hammer should fall
8. Charge the weapon and place on AUTO
9. Pull the trigger and hold it to the rear then cycle the bolt more than once
10. Release the trigger and pull it again, nothing should happen (auto sear is functioning)
11. Charge the weapon then pull the trigger again and the hammer should fall
12. Function check complete

Significant visual indicators
- Any checked, knurled or serrated surface
- Any movable lever or switch
- Pins with gripping surfaces
- Index marks (two lines that need to be aligned to disassembled (CZ 75)
- Recoil spring with ends of different diameters

Appendix E - PKM Stepanova Tripod Setup Steps

PKM Stepanova/Pannoneski Tripod Deployment Steps for deploying on level terrain for a seated position

1: Start with a working tripod in transport configuration

2: Unlock the front leg locking lever

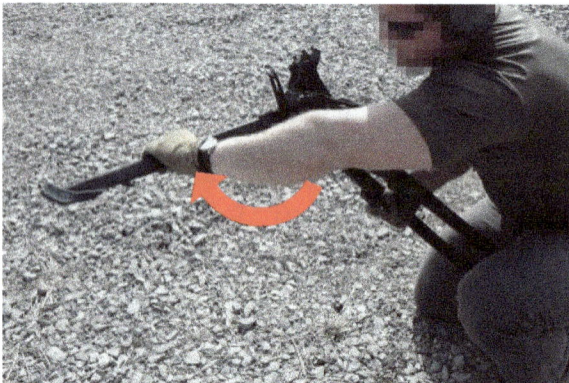

3: Fold out the front leg to the index point (on the tripod leg and base there are index lines, if not use a paint pen to make them)

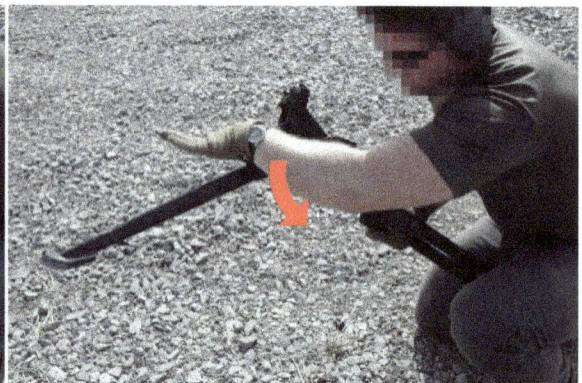

4: Lock the front leg locking lever

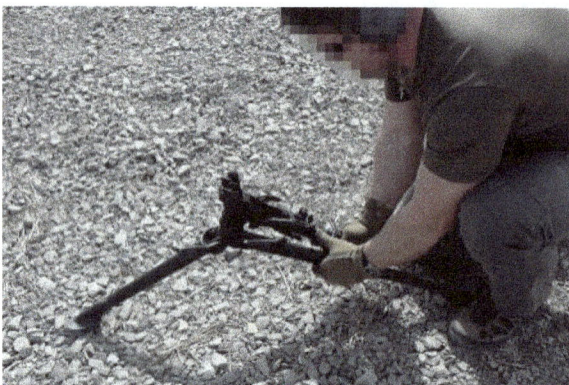

5: Set the tripod on the ground and rest on foot and leg to hold it upright

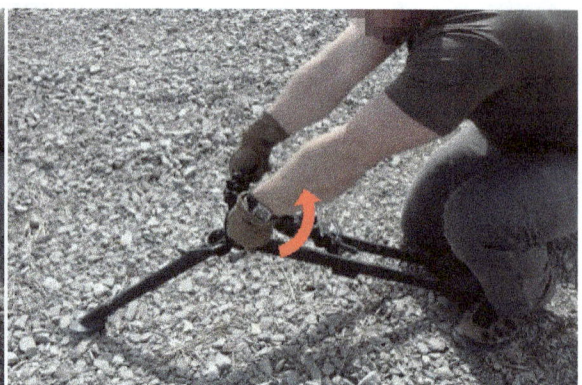

6: Unlock both rear leg locking levers

PKM Stepanova/Pannoneski Tripod Deployment Steps (continued)

7: Press the front leg into the ground so it does not slide

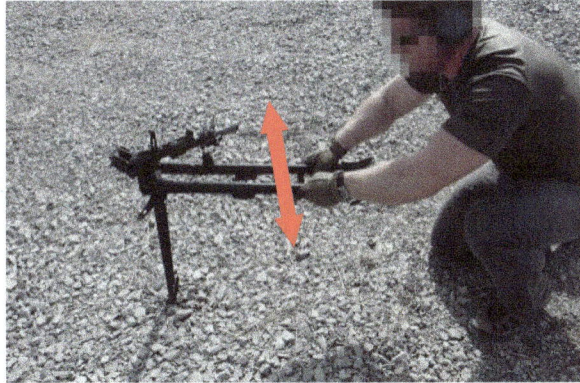

8: Spread the back legs to the full outward positions

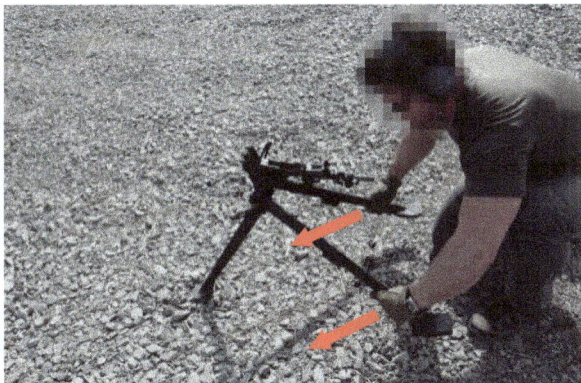

9: Once spread, while holding the front leg in the ground, adjust the rear legs down/forward two clicks

10: Set the tripod down without the rear legs moving

11: Lock the rear leg locking levers

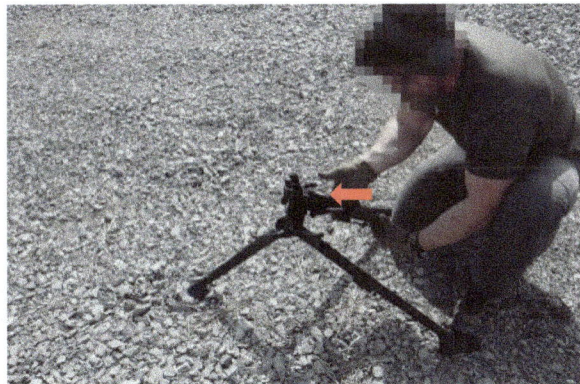

12: Unlock the Traverse/Elevation assembly from the cradle by pressing forward on the spring loaded lever on the right of the cradle

PKM Stepanova/Pannoneski Tripod Deployment Steps (continued)

13: Rotate the lower part of the T&E assembly under the tripod. Ensure the high angle fire portion of the T&E is folded up and over so it is not in the way.

14: Position the post receiver with a slight angle onto the post (ensure the receiver and post are clean)

15: Press slightly back and up to snap the receiver onto the post and ensure it is locked on

16: Level the cradle with the ground and lock the elevation lever down. This lever is on the left side of the T&E assembly, not the left rear leg locking lever.

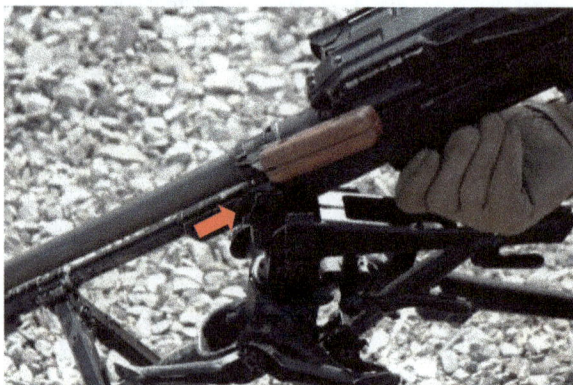

17: Position the mounting posts on both sides of the front of the PKM receiver into the cradle. The bipods will need to be in the down or forward position.

18: Lower the rear of the PKM and lock the front of the trigger guard into the rear of the cradle. You may need to press the spring loaded lever on the right of the cradle. Check that the gun is locked in.

PKM Stepanova/Pannoneski Tripod Deployment Steps (continued)

19: If the bipod was in the down position you may rotate them forward and lock them together or

20: You can fold the bipods back and snap them into the metal retainer clips on both sides of the cradle. An ammo can may be snapped onto the tripod depending on the height at which you have the tripod set.

The Tripod can be adjusted from prone to sitting to kneeling positions. The legs can also be adjusted individually depending on the terrain of the gun position.

Appendix F - PKM Stepanova Tripod Stowage Steps

PKM Stepanova Tripod Stowage Steps from being deployed on level terrain for a seated position.

1: Lower the bipod legs

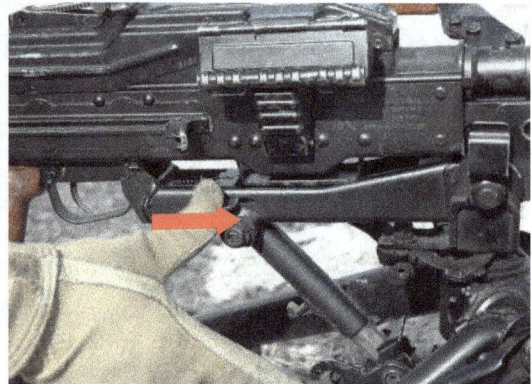

2: Unlock the front of the trigger guard from the rear of the cradle. You will need to press the spring loaded lever on the right of the cradle forward.

3: Lift up on the rear of the PKM and remove it from the tripod by pushing it forward out of the cradle and set it on the bipods.

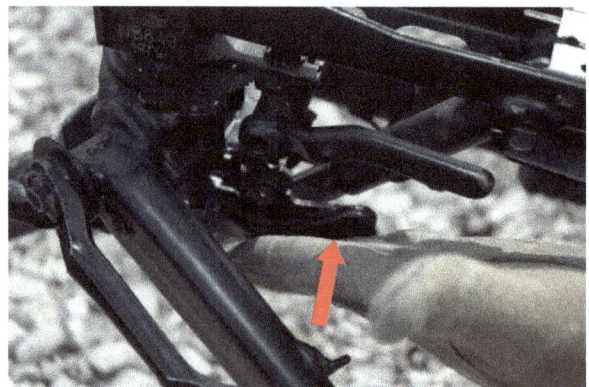

4: Unlock the elevation locking lever

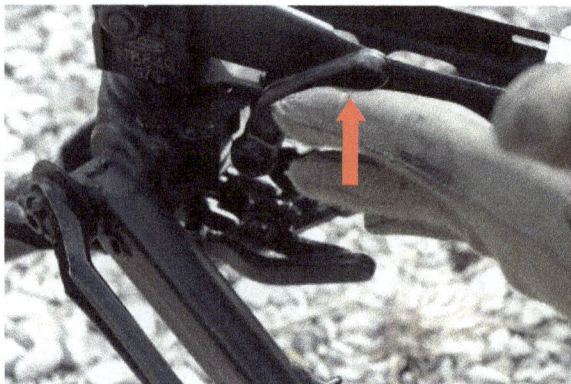

5: unlock the traverse locking lever, center the cradle and lock it back down

6: With your right hand reach in and unlock the T&E assembly from the post on the bottom of the tripod. There is a release which you use your right thumb to unlock this assembly, press on the latch and down to unlock.

PKM Stepanova Tripod Stowage Steps (continued)

7: Once unlocked now rotate the assembly back towards the rear of the cradle.

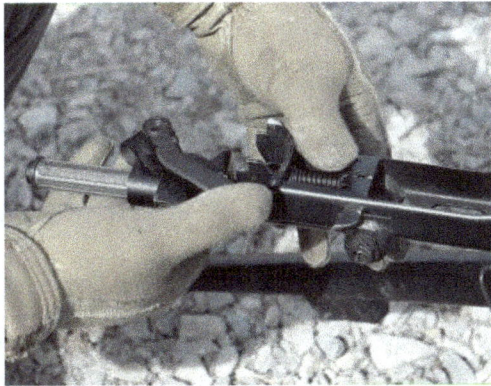

8: Rotate the lower part of the T&E assembly so the working parts are on the side

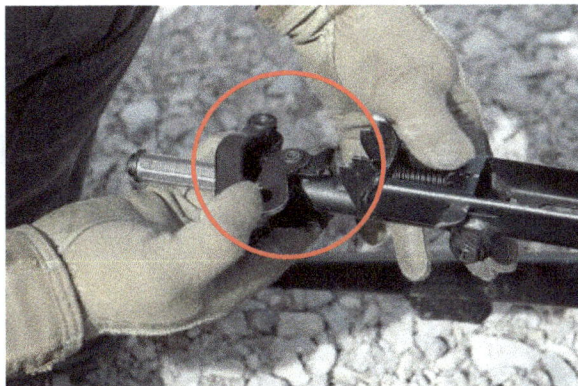

9: Lock the elevation locking lever to hold the working parts of the T&E assembly in place for stowage

10: Lock the T&E assembly to the rear of the cradle with the spring loaded lever on the right side

11: Unlock the front leg locking lever

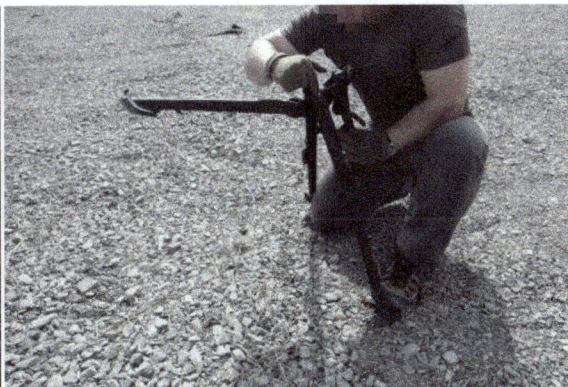

12: Lift the tripod front leg up with the rear legs firmly in the ground.

PKM Stepanova Tripod Stowage Steps (continued)

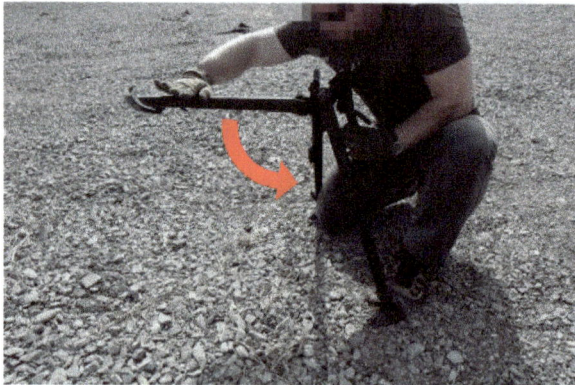

13: Fold back the front leg toward the rear legs

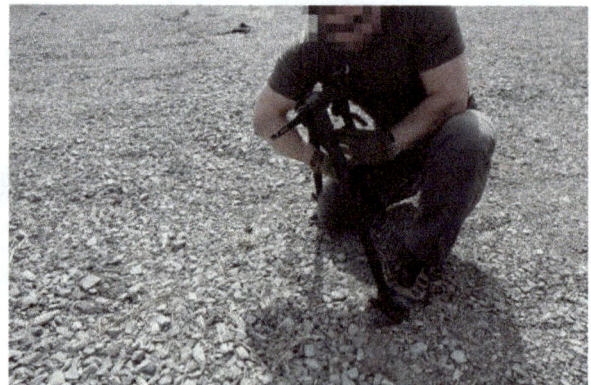

14: Once you have the front leg fully to the rear…

15: aim the spike on the front leg for the hole in the bottom of the T&E assembly. Once the spike is in the hole lock the front leg locking lever.

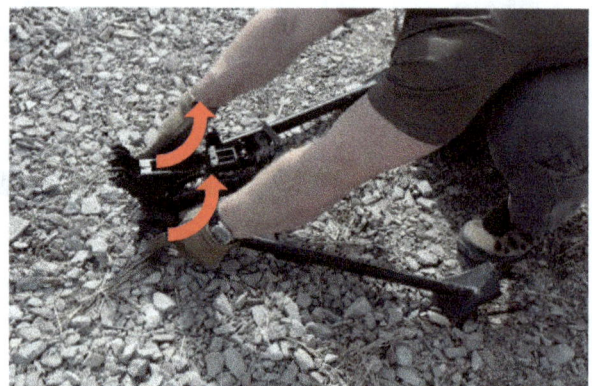

16: With the tripod on the ground, unlock both of the rear leg locking levers.

17: Once the rear leg locking levers are unlocked…

18: Grasp the rear legs

PKM Stepanova Tripod Stowage Steps (continued)

19: Press the rear legs in towards the center and front leg/cradle assembly.

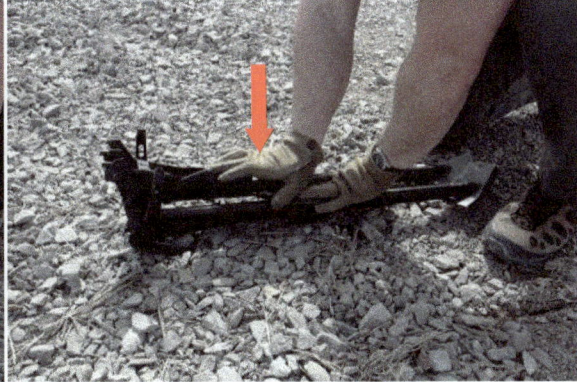

20: Press down on the tripod to bring the rear legs to their fullest upward position towards the cradle.

21: Lock both of the rear leg locking levers.

The tripod is now configured for transport or storage. If you place the tripod in the tripod bag do so by putting the feet of the legs in first so as not to damage the head of the cradle.

www.ingramcontent.com/pod-product-compliance
Lightning Source LLC
Chambersburg PA
CBHW080522110426
42742CB00017B/3205